From the Heart

Explorations in True Nature and Unconditional Love

ISBN – 979-8-6960-5794-1

Cover artwork by Paul Locke Art

www.paullock-art.com

Printed in the United Kingdom

Thank you for the glimpses

In loving memory of my dad,

I wish I'd listened more about the trees and birds.

John Oswell
1937 - 1999

For Will and Jack,

I'm so grateful and honoured to be your mum.
The world is a better place with you both in it.

CONTENTS

Contents

PART ONE

"All we are is peace, love and wisdom and the power to create the illusion that we're not."

Jack Pransky

Bringing the book to life

*"Do it badly; do it slowly; do it fearfully;
do it any way you have to, but do it."*
Steve Chandler

I'm so grateful that you are reading this sentence. It means that the book idea that found me in July 2020 has shown up in the world raising money for Heart Link Children's Charity. I'm also thrilled that the wonderful people in this book get to share with you their beautiful stories and insights about life.

In the middle of a global pandemic the idea for this booked showed up, unannounced and unprompted. To be honest I didn't have the time, energy or skills to write a book but despite me, the book was persistent. My first mistake was mentioning it to my partner. He loved the idea and wouldn't let me wriggle out of it, my usual habit when inspiration strikes. I then decided to write the book for a charity close to my heart, how could I not take action now? Finally, the idea that came to me, meant that other people had to contribute their time and love into writing their pieces so again this book held me to account, I couldn't let them down. As Steve says "Do it badly; do it slowly; do it fearfully; do it any way you have to, but do it." Which is what happened.

I'm so grateful for every one of these factors that pinned me down to my laptop for hundreds of hours so this book could express itself through me. I am deeply touched by what has shown up on the pages and I hope the messages will ripple out into the world at a time when love and understanding are much needed.

You will see that in part one of the book I give you some background to the glimpses that life gave me into true nature and unconditional love and the search that followed. Part two of the book is a compilation of other people's insights which provide such a rich diversity of life experiences but point to common understandings about the deeper aspects of life.

Much love,

Nicola x

Glimpses behind the curtain of life

1999

"If the doors of perception were cleansed every thing would appear to man as it is, Infinite. For man has closed himself up, till he sees all things thro' narrow chinks of his cavern."
William Blake

The telephone woke me with a start and dread overwhelmed me as I knew what this call meant. Moments later I'm driving to the hospital to say goodbye to my dad. I'd been fearing this day for six months, the sleepless nights worrying about my dad dying was playing out right in the moment.

I'd imagined torment and pain but instead I noticed the most peaceful sense of connection and love flow through me. It was a beautiful June morning; the sun was beginning to rise turning the sky into a breath-taking work of art.

I was curious about my peaceful experience and that I'd even noticed the beauty of the sunrise, given the circumstance. Then thinking fell away. Time stood still and, in an instant, everything was perfection and made of love, the road, the sky, me, my dad. Such immense peace, no separation just pure unconditional love – words are a blunt tool to describe the indescribable. True nature revealed itself as oneness or unconditional love.

This glimpse behind the curtain felt like a parting gift from my dad, I knew he had passed in that moment. The experience never left me, and that seed of curiosity lay dormant within me for years to come.

2002

"The discovery that peace, happiness and love are ever-present within our own Being, and completely available at every moment of experience, under all conditions, is the most important discovery that anyone can make."
Rupert Spira

I was lying in the bath paralysed by fear, my twelve-day old baby was having open heart surgery. Lying in the bath felt like the only thing I could do to keep myself together. It was the first time I'd been at home since giving birth and the reminders of the baby were everywhere apart from the bathroom. Hours later and I was walking across the intensive care unit to see my baby for the first time post-surgery. It was a huge room with so many strange noises, smells and sounds. I saw the surgeon's concerned expression and dread solidified in every cell of my body. As I neared my baby nothing could have prepared me for the sight of him surrounded by wires, tubes, and equipment. My senses were overwhelmed, and I could barely hear the surgeon as he talked about the operation and the importance of the next 24 hours. It was the most challenging experience I'd ever had to face, and it felt unbearable. I couldn't bear to think of my baby dying or being severely brain damaged, but my mind kept going to these scenarios. Fear and resistance continued to build with every beep of the machines and action of the medical team. I remember thinking about how I was going to make it through the next few hours.

Grace intervened and it felt like my thinking mind short circuited. I fell out of fear and landed in peace. The machines and the beeping faded into the background and pure presence revealed itself as the foreground. I wasn't living in the mind created story of what had happened, what could have happened or what might happen. The incessant fear based thinking of the last few hours stopped. When those stories went away what was left was this moment, peace, gratitude, and unconditional love.

Unconditional love meant I could be with my baby as he was in that moment without judgement. I knew in my being that he would be okay. Not that I knew that he was going to live but that I knew, come what may, the essence of his being would be okay, it was unbreakable. It was also known that this was the same for me and every human on the planet. In not needing him to live or for the situation to be different, for me to be okay, he and I were free to be exactly as we were. What we were turned out to be life expressing itself through pure unconditional love.

I was given a felt experience of this Rupert Spira quote, "The discovery that peace, happiness and love are ever-present within our own Being, and completely available at every moment of experience, under all conditions, is the most important discovery that anyone can make." I always thought that life had to be a certain way or that I had to do something to have peace and happiness. This deeper seeing showed me this wasn't the case and that peace and happiness are our true nature but we have a thinking mind that can veil this knowing and appear to take us away from it.

The thinking mind came back a few days later and I was once again in the grip of the ebb and flow of resistance and fear. I didn't share my experience with anyone because I was worried that stress had caused me to have a break from reality, I didn't understand the experience as the beautiful gift it was. It was years before I saw that this was a glimpse into the true nature of reality. Again, like the experience with my dad, I was left confused but curious, another seed was planted.

2006

"Your task is not to seek for love, but merely to seek and find all the barriers within yourself that you have built against it."
Rumi

The green hospital curtains were pulled around the bed, like a cocoon, as I gazed into the eyes of my new born baby. This time it was me hooked up to all sorts of wires following an emergency caesarean section. My baby also had some complications, but grace had appeared again and I found myself in a state of deep gratitude, acceptance and presence. All of the drama of the previous couple of days had melted away and what was left was love and connection. The hours slip by unnoticed as my baby and I fell into a natural rhythm of life planted in the now. Thoughts of the past and the future didn't arise or were not noticed and there was absolutely no resistance to what was happening. In that experience, everything was known to be just as it should be, the wires, the soreness, my babies condition were all the perfection of life showing up and not being interpretated by a thinking mind which thinks it knows just how things should really be.

My mind could have kicked up all sorts of resistance and suffering around another complicated birth, another baby needing specialist care, about the pain I was experiencing but for whatever reason that didn't show up and I was gifted a few days of pure love, of seeing something deeper about life.

As before, after a few days of this quiet mind the thinking mind came back online and with it the conditioning and concepts. The experience in the hospital was chalked up to be because

I was able to hold my baby and take care of him in a way, I hadn't had with my first child. But somewhere deep down another connection was forming.

The Search

*"Yesterday I was clever, so I wanted to change the world.
Today I am wise, so I am changing myself."*

"What you seek is seeking you."
Rumi

All three of these experiences, described in the previous chapter, were glimpses into the deeper reality of life. They didn't last but they left a faint remembrance which the mind couldn't understand, and words couldn't express. Life became busy raising two children and the experiences faded into the background, but looking back I now see that the search had begun.

I've always been interested in the human experience and had taken a psychology degree at university in my twenties. The human mind fascinated me, and my bookcase was full of psychology and self-help books. After the glimpses this intensified, and I started to search to make sense of the experiences.

In 2010, out of the blue, an event rocked my foundations, and I was thrown into deep fear, confusion and hurt. My life was turned upside down, for months the best I could do was take care of the children, go to work, and then collapse in bed willing sleep to take the pain and worry away. There were no glimpses into the deeper nature of life, and I was lost in the world of the thinking mind resisting and suffering. My mind would time travel to the past, going over and over my life to try to understand what had happened. It would then flip to a terrifying future where life wasn't okay, totally made up but experienced as real and true. I had wonderful support from my friends and family and eventually, the fear based mind lost its grip and things began to feel more manageable. What emerged from the embers of this situation was an intense seeking for truth.

My world was overtaken by the desire to understand the meaning of life and I left my secure job in education and began retraining as a business and personal coach and then as a psychotherapist. All of this training helped but it didn't explain what I'd seen about reality underneath the stories of the mind. During this time, I also threw myself into exploring quantum physics, spiritual teachings from the East and energy work, anything and everything!

Each new thing I would explore felt like it gave me a jigsaw piece to help create a more helpful picture. One day I was putting together a parent coaching course around wellbeing and I was searching on YouTube for content. It led me to an understanding of the mind called the 3 Principles or innate health, a lightbulb went on. This simple, but powerful, understanding helped me to understand how we are thinking beings and our experience is created from the inside out, not the outside in as we are taught. It also pointed to the deeper intelligence we are made of, the creative loving energy of life that is spinning the planet, creating oak trees from acorns, beating our hearts and growing our fingernails. Seeing this helped to shift a lot of confusion and led to some helpful insights into life. Life became so much simpler.

Soon after I discovered the teachings of non-duality and consciousness teachings. It became apparent that those glimpses I'd had were openings to a deeper spiritual truth or moments of being 'awake' to life. The seeds planted during those glimpses were being germinated by the light of awareness. I realised that we are so much more than the limited concepts we have about ourselves and others. I now believe that life is about waking up to these deeper truths and then playing the game of life from that place of deeper knowing. It's not only about the bliss of the glimpses or peak experiences but about finding the place inside which never changes. Coming home to the peaceful presence that we essentially are. At the same time embracing our humanness, with all of its quirks, and allowing the wisdom of life to unfold from a place of love.

In part two of this book my friends, clients and colleagues describe how they see life and share the insights that have changed their lives. It's my hope that part two will keep your thinking mind engaged but more importantly it will stir the knowing that you have, deep inside, about the nature of life too. This is not a how to guide and you won't get step by step instructions about how to have a better life. Rather it's about getting curious, it's about not knowing and questioning which will allow you space to explore yourself. I know that this is an exploration of a lifetime and in this life there is no end to the depth of understanding that can be uncovered.

> "We shall not cease from exploration
> And the end of all our exploring
> Will be to arrive where we started
> And know the place for the first time."
>
> T.S. Eliot

Reaching out for help

"And suddenly you know: It's time to start something new and trust the magic of new beginnings."
Meister Eckhart

The book idea was centred around collaboration with other people. I began reaching out to people, I knew, who themselves had experienced insights about the reality of life. I contacted over 150 people and had wonderful responses from people even when they felt that they couldn't contribute. To give you a better context to part two, below is a copy of a document I sent out to my contacts.

Hi,

I hope you are well.

An idea landed in my head from who knows where, I nearly ignored it but here I am writing to you.

My vision is to collate short responses from people who have had insights into the deeper nature of life and unconditional love.

I am reaching out to you and others, for some of your time, to see if we can breathe life into this idea. The idea will be an opportunity to spread love and understanding in the world and to raise money for charity at the same time.

My wonderful son will be 18 in August and this project would help to raise funds for a children's charity that supported my family when he was born with an undiagnosed heart condition that required open heart surgery.

That experience gave me a glimpse behind the curtain and ignited my love of truth. It seems so fitting now to have an opportunity to spread a strong message about true nature and unconditional love on a larger scale.

With your consent, responses would be collated into a book which will be sold to raise money for Heart Link Charity www.heartlink-glenfield.org.uk. I will also include some details of your business too i.e. website address or contact details.

If you would love to help, you can do this by answering these questions in a format that suits you;

1) What would you love the world to know about true nature and unconditional love?

2) How has this deeper seeing changed your world?

   Optional

3) What are you up to in the world? – A short bio, how can people connect with you/work with you?

4) A favourite quote to go at the top of your section in the book

I'm happy to get responses in a format that suits you, either;

1) Responding in writing and email it back to me info@hippocoaching.co.uk

2) Recording a video or audio of your replies (no longer than 15 minutes)

   - either something you record yourself or

   - we can chat on Zoom and I can ask you the questions directly

Please let me know what's best for you. I've set a deadline of Friday 7th August 2020 for responses in the hope I can have it published by my son's birthday at the end of August...

Thank you for considering the request. I look forward to hearing from you.

With all my love

Nicky

Nicky Drew
Psychotherapist & Coach
www.hippocoaching.co.uk   www.afreemind.co.uk
email – info@hippocoaching.co.uk

The brilliant creativity of life showed up in the wide variety of styles in the responses you will see. I wanted to let each individual's unique voice come through, so I have only lightly edited the written contributions. Video interviews are more heavily edited for ease of reading. I have also decided to keep original spelling and grammar from the contributor's so you will see English and US English throughout the book.

The Paths

*"We have the most wonderful job in the world. We find
people in various stages of sleep. And then we get to tap
them on the shoulder and be with them as they wake up to
the full magnificence of life."*
Sydney Banks

The contributors in this book come from all over the world,
New Zealand, Australia, Indonesia, Europe, Hawaii and North
America. They range in age from twenties to eighties. They
have a vast array of socio economic backgrounds and life
experiences. Some work in the helping professions, others
work in sports, trades and administration. Life has given each
of them an opportunity for insight into the deeper nature of the
human experience. Before or following these insights the
contributors have explored many paths in the self
development, psychological and spiritual fields. Many have
come across an understanding of the human experience
called the 3 Principles or innate health and/or also the field of
non-duality. Below is a brief outline of these understandings
to give some context to some of the stories that follow. It is
my belief that no particular path or indeed any path is required
for true nature and unconditional love to be revealed. But it
certainly seems that seeking to understand does happen for
lots of people and that these two understanding help people
to uncover what is not true and point them in a more helpful
direction.

The 3 Principles
Sydney Banks was a Scottish born welder living in Canada
when in 1973 he had a profound insight into the nature of the
human experience. He went from being angry and insecure to
peaceful and content. Syd began sharing his understanding

and with the help of clinical psychologists developed the field of psychology which he called the 3 Principles. The Principles are Mind, Consciousness and Thought and the understanding points people to the creation of experience through the power of Thought and to the deeper seeing of the wisdom or innate intelligence which is our true nature.

Syd wrote a number of books and travelled the world lecturing to the public, doctors, psychiatrists, psychologists, schools and to prison inmates. Syd's work is still being shared across the world, having a profound impact on those it touches. Lots of evidence based research has and is being carried out in businesses, education settings and rehabilitation and prison settings. You will read transformational stories in this book from contributors describing profound shifts in their experience of life after coming across this understanding. I have provided links for more information at the end of the book.

Non-duality
Non-duality is a spiritual teaching or understanding. The word 'Non-duality' is a translation of the Sanskrit word 'Advaita', which means 'not two'. It points to the oneness of life, to the true nature of consciousness underneath the human experience. It points to "A wholeness which exists here and now, prior to any apparent separation. It's a word that points to an intimacy, a love beyond words, right at the heart of present moment experience. It's a word that points us back Home. And despite the compelling appearance of separation and diversity there is only one universal essence, one reality. Oneness is all there is – and we are included." Jeff Foster.

Non-duality is an exploration of who we really are, both the formless essence and the conditioned form. For me it has been about seeing the nature of conditioning and the habits of the conceptual mind to divide, fix and label. When we get lost in the form we suffer, we feel lost and are driven by fear, continually trying to secure ourselves. When we begin to look towards the formless we see that awareness or consciousness is who we really are and the insecure habits of mind can begin to drop away. I have provided links for more information at the back of the book.

PART TWO

*"When we have reached the outposts of the mind,
we are ready for the journey to the heart."*

Francis Lucille

Michael Neill

*"You have a wisdom inside you – listen for it. You have a
light inside you – feel its glow. You have the power to speak
and act and make things manifest in the world – let your
wisdom and light guide you as you do."*
Michael Neill

Interview

What would you love the world to know about true nature and
unconditional love?

What I'd love the world to know about true nature is its
vastness - it's not small!

I was reading something saying that if you took seven billion
mason jars and you filled each one of them with ocean water,
you wouldn't put a dent in the ocean. You could study and
analyze the nature of what was in the jar and you could go
okay, well, it's got this much salt and it's got this much that
etc. Even inside the mason jar it would have properties of its
true nature, observable and measurable and tangible, but its'
true, true nature is way beyond that which is measurable in
any jar.

I liked it as a metaphor, because when you take the water out
of the ocean, you disconnect it from the tides, you disconnect
it from the whole, and study it in isolation. But that doesn't take
into account that there's a movement inside us that is always
moving towards the whole, and there's a larger intelligence
behind the whole. And so, the return to our true nature is not
studying what's in the jar. It's pouring what's in the jar back
into the ocean. And then you can get a sense of true nature

and the vastness of it, the laws by which it operates, and what's moving it.

You will never find that particular configuration again no matter how many jars you scoop. The content of every jar is both temporary and unique. Yet every jar is taken from the whole, and every jar will return to the whole. And so, what I'd love the world to see is that true nature is not "your" true nature as opposed to "my" true nature. It is the true nature of life for every human being on the planet.

It is vast beyond comprehension, though we can kind of intuit it a bit. I find most people kind of know what I mean when I talk about it. But if they think about it too hard, it goes out the window. So in a way, instead of trying to understand it conceptually, the easiest way to find it is to get rid of everything that isn't it. I'm not literally recommending this, people, but set your life on fire and whatever doesn't burn is real!

In a book of Zen wisdom called the Xinxin Ming, the patriarch Seng T'san says "Do not seek the truth; only cease to cherish opinions." If you keep letting go of all of your ideas about life and self, at some point you'll begin to glimpse what might be true beyond all ideas. And it's the same with unconditional love - the easiest way to find it is to let go of anything that isn't it. Statements like 'I love you if', 'I love you when', 'I love you as long as', 'I am worthy of love if', 'I am worthy of love when', 'I am worthy of love as long as', etc. are the conditions we place on love. So with all those conditions in place, love becomes a currency that we can trade for with good behavior. And it's kind of a shitty currency. I mean, it is accepted most places, but the exchange rates are pretty fierce.

The best description I ever heard of unconditional love came from a book by the Christian writer Philip Yancey. He was talking about God and unconditional love and he wrote, "…there is nothing we can do to make God love us more.... there is nothing we can do to make God love us less." To this day, that's my favorite description of unconditional love. I can't do anything to get more of it. I can't do anything to get less of it. It works a bit like gravity. I could worship the gods of gravity and I will not get one ounce more or less gravity than somebody who worships the anti-gravity gods. I will not have any more or less gravity than somebody who doesn't know gravity exists. It is unconditional - literally without conditions.

We tend to think about love as this noble thing that must be earned, but to me it seems like it's just what's always already there without all the filters, and limits, and edges, and if/thens, and concepts, and implications, and applications.

I did a radio show on the power of unconditional love once. And I was talking about the nature of it, that we're swimming in it. And a woman phoned in the next week, and she said, "Yeah, I tried that unconditional love thing you talked about with my husband last week and it didn't work. What else you got?"

Now I'm going to go out on a limb and say that was not unconditional love. That was tactical love, and it didn't work because it doesn't work. Using the gravity metaphor again, gravity never doesn't work. Right? And it's not a tactic, like, "I'm going to use gravity on them." You can't "use" it, but it's always there and you can take it into account. It isn't about you, it isn't up to you, you cannot diminish it, and you cannot expand it. You cannot become less worthy of it or more worthy of it in a meaningful way. Because it simply 'is'. And so, I think if people start to see love 'is', full stop, end of sentence, there are a lot of things we've learned to do in our lives that would start to fall away. And we would experience a lot more freedom, and perhaps obviously a lot more love.

How has this deeper seeing for you changed your world?

I stress a lot less. I worry a lot less. I take myself a lot less seriously, but not in a bad way. I think people sometimes think that the opposite of seriousness is frivolity, but I would say it's quite the contrary. In one of his talks, the Scottish mystic Syd Banks said "...people complain that I'm not serious enough, that I laugh too much. But they don't understand, I'm serious too. But without the feeling."

In other words, I can take something seriously without taking it seriously -without the heaviness that people associate with it. I can treat something with respect without treating it as if it ultimately has a power it doesn't have.

So, for me given the question, yeah, my life's a lot nicer and a lot lighter. But I notice with interest it's no less impactful. If anything, I've become more engaged in the world, but in a very different way than I was trying to before. Not from guilt, not from shame, not from an attempt to be a good person, not because I think "things are so horrible and they must be stopped".

Here's an example. We live in an area with lots of woods, and from time to time there are trees across the road. And if they aren't completely blocking the road, what most people do is they drive around them. And there's certainly times I've done that. But there are also times when I'm not in a hurry, when I'm not overwhelmed, when it's not all too much, where I'll pull the car over and drag the tree off the road. Not because it makes me a better person, but because it's just the obvious thing to do.

I think being able to not be overwhelmed by the heaviness and self-importance of your thinking lets you just handle what's in front of you as best you can. That's been a real gift to me as somebody who used to stress about everything, worry about everything, try to control everything, try to make everything happen in just the right way, and then feel bad when I couldn't. Which I guess makes me a happily recovering control freak!

About Michael Neill
Michael Neill is an internationally renowned author, speaker, and thought leader, challenging the cultural mythology that stress and struggle are a prerequisite to creativity and success. His bestselling books, podcasts, keynotes, trainings, and retreats have inspired and impacted millions of people on six continents around the world.

Michael's mission is to unleash the human potential with intelligence, humor, and heart, and his unique brand of loving disruption has made him a beloved catalyst and creative sparkplug to CEOs, leaders, creative artists, and anyone who wants to get more out of themselves and their lives while making more of a difference in the world.

His TEDx talks 'Why Aren't We Awesomer?' and 'Can a TEDx Talk Really Change the World?' have been viewed by nearly two million people, and his blog and podcast, Caffeine for the Soul, is now in its 19th year and going strong…
www.michaelneill.org

Mavis Karn

"There is no situation that is not transformable. There is no person who is hopeless. There is no set of circumstances that cannot be turned about by ordinary human beings and their natural capacity for love of the deepest sort."
Archbishop Desmond Tutu

When I asked Mavis if she'd like to contribute to my book, she offered to let me share a beautiful letter she wrote titled 'The Secret'. Below, Mavis explains how the letter came about.

On the last day of my two-year project teaching kids in prison about who they really are inside, (full of potential and naturally possessed of everything they need), they had a party for me.

I loved them all so much and wanted to give them something from my heart, so I wrote this letter. The letter eventually found its way to an artist imprisoned in a men's facility who made a poster out of it to share within the prison community.

The Secret

Dear Kids (and former kids),

I have a secret to tell you, Nobody meant to keep it from you...It's just that it's been one of those things that's so obvious that people couldn't see it...like looking all over for the key that you have in your hand.

The secret is that you are already a completely whole, perfect person. You are not damaged goods, you are not incomplete, you are not flawed, you are not unfinished, you do not need remodeling, fixing, polishing or major rehabilitation. You already have within you everything you need to live a wonderful life. You have common sense, wisdom, genius creativity, humor, self-esteem…you are pure potential…you are missing nothing.

The only thing that can keep you from enjoying all that you already are is a thought. One thought, your thought. Not someone else's thought. Your thought . . . Whatever thought you are thinking at the moment that feels more important to think than feeling grateful, alive, content, joyful, optimistic, loving and at peace. . . that's the only thing that's between you and happiness.

And guess who's in charge of your thinking? Guess who gets to decide where your attention goes? Guess who gets to write, produce, direct and star in the moment you're in the middle of? You! Just you. Not your past (stored thought), not the future (did you ever notice that it never, ever shows up?), not your parents (they all think their own thoughts), or your friends (ditto), or school or television or situations or circumstances or anything else. Just you.

Thinking is an awesome capability. Like any capability it can be used either as a tool or as a weapon against ourselves and others. And just like with any other tool, we can tell whether we're using it for or against ourselves by how it feels. When we think against ourselves or others, we get in trouble. When we don't, we usually stay out of trouble.

FEELINGS EXIST TO WARN US AWAY FROM USING OUR THINKING TO CREATE TROUBLE IN OUR LIVES AND TO GUIDE US BACK TO OUR NATURAL, HEALTHY ABILITY TO LIVE OUR LIVES TO THE FULLEST.

So, please remember that your thoughts are not always telling you the truth. When we're in low moods, feeling down, our thoughts are not be trusted...our IQ drops. When our thoughts pass and we lighten up, our thinking is once again creative, positive...our IQ goes up. The only way you can feel badly about yourself and your life is if you think badly about them...it's up to you, every single minute you're alive. It's always up to you! This is the best, most liberating secret I ever learned, and I want you to know it too.

With love, Mavis

About Mavis Karn
Mavis Karn LSW, MA is a counselor and educator in St. Paul, Minnesota. She has spent the last 40+ years doing her work with individuals, agencies. hospital, prisons, businesses, families, athletes, etc. She has taken her work to South Africa, as well as on-line with people from all over the USA and beyond. Mavis can be contacted at mavis.karn@aol.com

Maria Wood

"Who'd have thought it could be so simple? That love is what makes all the difference. It doesn't cost anything and it doesn't have a negative effect. There isn't a single problem that can't be solved from love."

Extract from Love for Free from Daily Yarns: Riding the Lockdown Roller Coaster of Emotions by Maria Iliffe-Wood

Life in Between the Trains

There was a point a few years ago when life got too much for me. The doctor called it depression. He told me it was a mental illness that had been brought on by grief and anxiety.

I caved into a thick black cloud that enveloped my soul. I surrendered to the demons in my mind, believed that I was broken and stopped participating in life. If someone had told me then that I was unconditional love, and that I had a wisdom that would guide me through the dark days and nights, I think I would have punched their lights out. Except I was too polite. But I would have written them off as a crackpot.

When I look back at that time, I see the chinks of light, the moments when I was moved to take small tentative steps before I slumped back, exhausted, into the chair where I remained for the rest of the day, every day for three and a half months.

The chinks of light were the times when I picked up the phone and called the doctor. When I asked him about how I would come off the medication, even before I would let him prescribe it and all the times when I visited a friend who held my hand

and listened to me cry. They may not seem like much, but let me tell you, those things are BIG.

Those are tho moments when wisdom guided me, even though I had no clue that's what it was. These were the instants when a crack appeared amid the noise of my thinking and true nature and unconditional love were able to break through and inch me forward until I was ready to take bigger steps and move back into the flow of life.

Even after my depression, I wasn't in the flow. Life was still an uphill struggle, I still carried a backpack stuffed full of rocks called low self-worth, anxiety and expectation. I had all the outward signs of a successful life, like a nice house, fast car and all the material accoutrements that made it look like my life was enviable, but my inner life was still in turmoil.

I came out of those few months stronger and more resilient and with a renewed energy but the battle in my head carried on.

You know the one. The fight that goes with having the impossible expectation that I need to be a perfect human being. The fight to prove to the whole world that I was good enough whilst always knowing that was a war that I couldn't win. The fight to reach the bar that I'd set so high that I could never achieve it. And every time I fell short, I would crucify myself for the fact of not being good enough. That battle.

All this added up to a level of noise in my mind that I had become accustomed to. Comfortable with, in the same way that I'd got used to the noise of trains every five minutes when I lived next door to a railway station.

I was not born with this noise in my head. It was something that I learned and that had built up over the first forty years of my life.

As I write this now, I know that there's a truth that sits at the heart of who I am. I close my eyes and I feel a groundswell of warm emotions, that emanate from my core. I imagine this is how I felt when I was a young child, when I was free, when I was uninhibited by any sense of shame or guilt, when life was just something I lived, not something I thought about.

It's how I used to feel before the formation of my thinking, in a time when I had no words. When I didn't need to explain it, yet the energy of life flowed through me, unresisted.

This is how I felt before I learned to be self-conscious and judge and criticize and berate myself for not living up to my own impossible standards, because then expectation was not a word that existed in my awareness.

It's what life was like before I started to live in a pool of angst and anxiety, that came when I learned to believe that I was not good enough.

It's what life was like in between the trains. The quiet stillness before the next train of thought arrived like a storm in a teacup, to blow away my serenity. I paid attention to the trains and ignored the quiet times in between and the space in which the noise was located.

It is what life is like when I stand and watch the train and know that I am not it.

What do I want people to know about true nature and unconditional love? Well it's how we were born and it never goes away, no matter what we think. That true nature and unconditional love is an eternal pool of wisdom that we float in, when we remember that we don't need to swim against the tide, and it's always here whenever we need it, whether we believe that to be true or not.

That which the doctor's called depression, a mental illness, I now see as my true nature giving me a break from my inner turmoil. It invited me to stop, recoup and regenerate and gave me strength, so that I could continue to carry the heavy load until such a time as I realised that I didn't need to carry it anymore. When I did that, I put the backpack down and I knew I'd found the key to a happy life.

I know now that a successful life is not what I have or what I do, or how well I do it, it's who I am. And I wish that everyone could see that too.

About Maria Iliffe-Wood
I'm Maria Iliffe-Wood. I'm a coach and I work with leaders, other coaches and writers to help them to grow beyond model, theories, tools and techniques. I have written two books, the first for coaches, called Coaching Presence: Building Consciousness and Awareness into Coaching Interventions and the more recent one Daily Yarns: Riding the Lockdown Roller Coaster of Emotions. I have another book called A Caged Mind, on the go, which I hope to publish in the next twelve months. You can read more of my writing at www.iliffe-wood.co.uk and find out about my work at www.fromquiet.co.uk.

Wyn Morgan

*"The wisdom humanity seeks lies within the consciousness
of all human beings, trapped and held prisoner by their own
personal minds."*
Sydney Banks from the Missing Link

True nature and Unconditional love

Understanding my true nature as a human being had been a
life changer for me. For the first 42 years of my life, I'd been a
very serious thinker. And that was the only thing between me
and seeing my true nature.

What was especially serious was the thinking I had about
myself, which was a habit that took me into bouts of
depression since I was very young. Having such a low opinion
of myself, I looked hard at all the things I thought that were
wrong with me – which of course had the inevitable result of
me feeling even worse about myself! I'd discount or dismiss
the things I might have liked about myself, they seemed
irrelevant to me because I wanted to fix what I thought was
wrong. And regardless of how much I was loved by my family,
I couldn't really hear nor feel it.

I remember taking the bus into the city centre of Swansea
every Saturday to buy a new 7-inch single and to look around
the record and clothes shops. While walking through the new
shopping centre through the crowds of strangers, I would
often well up, thinking I was odd, an outsider, alone and
broken. My eyes would water up of embarrassment and I'd
hold my head low. When I went to secondary school from the
age of 12, my academic results shot up and I was finding
something to be proud of - my intellect and academic ability.

Being towards the very top in every subject in the top class in each year gave me the biggest confidence boost and I remember walking through those same crowds in the same shopping centre on those Saturdays with my head held high, for the first time. That would set off a different precedent that kept me away from looking at my true nature, I thought my value as a human came from achievement. Academic achievement to career progression, business results within the companies I worked for, recognition from my peers and superiors were my new go-to in order to feel good about myself. And sometimes, it worked. I'd get that hit of external validation. Which naturally enough led me to wanting more hits – success and recognition became a drug and felt lost and down without them.

Through this, my career was progressing really well, and had my dream job of flying all over the world helping develop people in large organisations become more effective at sales, leadership, negotiation, facilitation, global contracting and so forth. Yet, my life and job only looked cool from the outside: most of the time it certainly didn't feel like that on the inside.

In my years of seeking to find what was wrong with me through therapists, coaches and NLP masters, I stumbled across someone who had begun working in a whole new way. I was sitting in his home in Los Angeles, having gone there hoping to be 'fixed' once and for all! He was so dismissive on the stories in my head and I was quite agitated at this person effectively telling me I'd made it all up and I was OK by nature. Not what I wanted to hear at the time, and I didn't hear it. But still, something shifted. "Wouldn't it be a shame to have a really cool life and not know it?" was something I was told that afternoon; and my counter-thought was "Yes, but I can't have a cool life being me!" That's how tied I was to the story I had about me at the time.

18 months later, I'd seen something during the most amazing 6-months of training I'd had; and on the final day we were all asked to say what we've become grateful of knowing since the 60 of us began the training. I said "I'm grateful for knowing I'm not my thinking", and passed the mic to the person sitting next to me, and around the room the mic went, each person sharing what they were grateful for. I barely listened to them. I was still puzzled by what I'd just said, because I'd known it to be 100% true for the first time – I am not who I think. And I am not what I think.

All those hundreds of thousands of thoughts that I'd had about me over the previous 42 years were nothing but a thought that looked real. Yet, I'd really seen that I can think ANYTHING, and so many of those thoughts I'd had I did not take seriously, see them as true, think more and more about them until they looked like my identity. I'd made the whole thing up! I make things up all the time! That's what every human does! Things began to crash in a wonderful way in this woeful story of who I thought I was.

Now, I see more and more that when I feel low, it means the relationship I have with low quality thinking is 'off' – I'm taking what I think as true, meaningful, permanent and personal when they are the opposite of those things: illusory, arbitrary, transient and universal for all human beings.

I can see that thought is an incredible energy of creation in human beings, and our ability to believe what we think is one characteristic that defines us as a species. We imagine all the time, including imagining our true nature is 'wrong'.

A quick client example with someone I spoke with a few weeks ago following her recent promotion to the board of a large packaged goods company. She was telling me all about her doubts about herself, her ability to do this new role, the credibility she thought she would lack in the boardroom and so on – the perfect storm of what's often called 'imposter syndrome'. I asked her:

"Do you ever think about what to have for dinner when you get home?" She looked at me rather dismissively through the video call screen and said

"Yes, what's that got to do with anything?"

"Do you then keep thinking about it and worry about what's for dinner and think, 'If I don't know what's or dinner, I'm a terrible person?'"
"No of course I don't!"
"Why not?"

"That would be crazy!" we were both chuckling at this point although she was still a bit bemused at what on earth I was getting at.

"Well, what makes the thought of you in your new job more real or worthy of attention compared with the thought of tonight's dinner?"

"They're totally different" she said, "One is real, I need help with and the dinner thought is clearly just something that comes into my head and goes"

"What is it about them that makes them different?"

"The feeling and how real each of them is!"

"How do you KNOW one is more real than the other?"

"I just do – isn't that obvious?"

"Well, let's take a look. In their essence, they're both thoughts, right?"

"Yes"

"How do we decide which one is more real and requires attention / fixing and worry?"

"I decide, I suppose. How...by thinking... wait! I decide, and that's a thought too??" A long pause and a pensive, reflective look showed up on my screen.

"So, what you're saying is, all this stuff is just things I've made up to seem important and worthy of worry"

"What do you think?"

"That's blown my mind a bit... I got this promotion on merit, I know that. Everyone on the board were in the decision making committee to promote me; so what have I been so worried about?!?" And she just relaxed.

Regardless of how pervasive and persuasive the thoughts appear to be we have about ourselves, they are not who we are. When I saw this, as the lady above started to get a glimpse of, I realised more and more about my true nature – and the true nature of every single human being.

One of my favourite questions about this true nature right now to ponder is this one: 'Who am I before I think of me?'

And how it looks to me today is this

I am energy and matter in the dance of being human for a short period of time.

The life-force energy that animates me is as timeless as the energy that created everything in the universe. Yes, created everything in the universe.

The 'matter' of me: every single cell in my body, every molecule, every atom, every sub-atomic particle was once something else, and will return to something else. My human form is temporary, yet timeless.

What my human form is made of, by astrophysics fact, is stardust. What's in me and all of me was made from an exploding star, billions of years ago.

So my true nature, and your true nature and the true nature of all of us is stardust animated by the energy that created stars, planets and light. And the fact that we are aware and conscious entities is, to me, like the universe's gift to itself: being aware of the wonder and beauty of everything on the earth and in the cosmos.

It is a wonder to me that the creative energy of thought is also the only thing that can hide me from my true nature – when I forget the nature of that thought energy!

I used to want to feel okay, then I saw I was okay when I saw I'm not my thinking. Now I see my true nature is far beyond okay when I see more and more about life itself.

It's also true to me that what is visible before my thinking (or when I see through thought's illusory nature) is love. Unconditional love.

I saw this really clearly one Sunday morning a few years ago. I was on my annual February pilgrimage to the Pacific Northwest of the US, where every February for a number of years around 70 people gather to rest and learn more from three pioneers and prominent teachers on the truth of who we are by nature. We come from all over the world for four days to see more deeply the truth of the discoveries of Sydney Banks for ourselves and then go back into our lives to help others see their own true nature. I was sharing a beautiful home overlooking the beautiful Skagit Bay inlet of the Pacific Ocean with six colleagues who had become friends and extended family.

From Thursday through to Saturday, I had morning calls with clients back in the UK and Europe, which meant getting up at 5.30am and routinely making a big pot of coffee for me and my friends ready for them when they would get up a few hours after me. Then on this Sunday, no calls. No need to get up at 5.30am. I had the luxury of not needing to get up until 8am. The body clock being what a body clock does, I was wide awake before 6am and really wanted a cup of coffee, so I made my way into the kitchen to make the usual big pot for all of us.

On this day, instead of retreating back to my room for calls, I took my comforting mug onto the deck overlooking the bay and breathed in the beauty of this familiar, yet still awesome beauty. I lent on the deck and stared for quite a while, counting my blessings of what I'd seen about me and my true nature. Gratitude poured from inside me and I felt so home, so peaceful and truly content.

Then a bird tweeted close to me. And tweeted again. A piecing tweet that broke my inner peace. I was having such a gorgeous moment, how dare this noise ruin it! What was this bird that was ruining my morning from over my right shoulder? After a brief respite and just as I was getting back to that beautiful feeling, the tweet came again, this time from a slightly different place. The bird had moved – I wanted to see it to chastise it, or at least give it a disdainful glare. It tweeted again; I still couldn't see it. Again it moved and the next tweet came from over to my left this time and seemingly closer. "Has this bird got it in for me or something?" I thought. Another quiet minute or so and there it was again – that tweet, down to my left. I looked and I saw the culprit of ruining my peace, a beautiful sparrow standing on the driveway next to the deck. And as soon as I saw the sparrow, I melted. I melted and loved the sparrow. It tweeted again, the identical bird, the identical sound – and I loved it. I saw the sparrow and the sound for what it was, not what I'd made up in my head about it. And what was underneath what I'd made up was love.

The next moment I saw the whole past five minutes with perspective and saw clearly that unconditional love is always, always, underneath my thinking. Sparrows tweet, dogs bark, cats meow, humans do human things. When I'm not in my judgemental, my personal thinking, they're doing what they do. I saw that if I don't love something or someone, it means I don't understand them. And as soon as I do understand them, like the beautiful innocent sparrow that Sunday morning, I love them. And, because conditions can only come from personal thought, unconditional love is the default setting. I would also say that I see unconditional love is the essence of pure consciousness. Pure consciousness untainted by personal thought.

Seeing that as true for myself has been a huge gift. Anyone or anything I'm resisting means one thing – I'm not seeing it purely and cleanly. I do not have to do anything from there. Touching that truth has had a long-lasting and beautiful impact on my experience of being alive.

About Wyn Morgan
Wyn Morgan is a change agent based in Windsor, UK and works with corporations and private individuals in every

continent around the world. He has been in the people development world for the past 20+ years within organisations, and as a coach-consultant with his own business for the past 14 years. His consistent track record of transforming clients and step-changing corporate results have made his a sought after resource. He has studied with Michael Neill and been mentored by George and Linda Pransky, Barb Patterson and Elsie Spittle. "I am constantly amazed how much more there is to see and how much more wondrous and simple life can actually be" "Helping my own clients in the corporate world achieve better results through the brilliance of their people along with those clients who come to me for their own personal needs is such a joy. I love watching them wake up to who they really are" Wyn says.

Website: www.wynning.co.uk e-mail: info@wynning.co.uk

Stef Cybichowski

"And in this game of life, we all search for ourselves. When I say selves, I mean inner selves, the thing that created the life in the first place. Now consciously, most of us are not aware of this. But if you're searching for happiness, if you're searching for tranquility, if you're searching just to have a nice, peaceful, loving, understanding life… in actual fact, you're searching for your inner self."
Syd Banks

Sydney Banks said: "Love is always the answer", one of the many explanations is that because beyond our conditioned, insecure, habitual personal thinking is an infinitely deeper realm of existence that most people are unaware of, but if it was understood, would transform their experience of ourselves, our relationships, our work, of being alive.

It is a space within us that is constant, eternal, it does not come and go, as does the content of our contaminated personal thought system.

When we touch this space beyond the illusion of personal thought, there is already love, connection, understanding, joy, compassion, peace, clarity, creativity, and we are beautifully guided by life. We don't need to find it, it is already there.

Because this part of us does not come and go, you could say it is our essence, the foundation we can rely on, when our true nature is love, it is what we are made of. We are the energy of life flowing through us in every moment.

We drop into this feeling of love, this 'who we really are' naturally when our flow of negative thinking falls away, when there is a moment of quietness, when there is stillness, we already know this on a deeper non-intellectual level, we just forget from time to time.

That is why Sydney Banks would say that "love is always the answer", because from the space of who we really are, we see ourselves and the world differently, we see it as it really is and we can respond to life with clarity and love, with the wisdom of life itself, beyond our own limited, judgemental thinking, 'right action' occurs and life flows. It is mysterious and beautiful. It is the place of miracles. All the answers we seek, everything every person on this earth is looking for is already within us. How perfect is that?

How has this deeper seeing changed your world?

Understanding on a deep level that unconditional love is who we are at source has allowed me to see the world with fresh, compassionate, heartfelt perspective.

I am less inclined to be as judgemental and critical. There is way more kindness, care and compassion.

Because of this, my experience of relationships has dramatically improved, with my late father, my sister, my son.

Even in times of difficulty and getting lost in thought, there is now a different relationship to my feelings, a sense (at some point) of "hold on, something is not right with this picture" and then eventually, I'm guided back to loving presence. There is such grace to the intelligence of the Universe.

About Stef Cybichowski
I consider myself so privileged to share the 3 Principles understanding with human beings from all walks of life through coaching, teaching, mentoring, public speaking in North

America, Latin America, China, The Middle East and Europe. Everywhere from Corporations, Schools, Mental Health Organisations and Private Individuals. Syd Banks said: "We have the best job in the world, wo get to tap people on the shoulder and watch as they wake up to the full magnificence of who they are."

My email address is stef@yourunlimitedpotential.co.uk, or my facebook page: 'Your deepest potential'

Jacqueline Hollows

"For in the true nature of things, if we rightly consider, every green tree is far more glorious than if it were made of gold and silver."
Martin Luther

I walk around with filters. The world I see is displayed on my internal dashboard through the lenses of my judgements and bias's and opinions. And what's worse is I apply those filters to myself! Comparing myself, contrasting my experience, judging my behaviour, my looks, my words, my body. It's exhausting!

In 2013 I discovered that there is something deeper than those lenses, deeper than the thing I see in the mirror, deeper than the judgements. Every year in the UK there is a Recovery Walk which is a celebration of people who are in recovery from any form of mental anguish, including addiction and alcoholism. I was volunteering for someone at that Walk by interviewing people along the way for a film he was making.

When we got to the park, I took a moment to let it all sink in after I finished interviewing a lady on the bench who happened to live nearby and just came to see what was going on. "It's just been lovely" she said. I stood at the edge of the grass of the park with the sunshine lighting up every corner of life, every blade of grass. The trees seemed to sparkle. The park was imbued with a magical aura that made everything beautiful. The music from the bandstand filled the air with songs of hope and joy and connection. Every space around the edges of the park had been utilized by stalls selling cakes, coffee, burgers, games and information. Little groups of people sat around on the green grass chatting and laughing.

I could feel the warmth from my purple 'Recovery Walk' polo shirt and long black trousers, hiding my bulging recovering knee. My hand felt hot and sweaty from holding the microphone. "Thank you." I said. And in that moment, it seemed I was filled up with light and love and sunshine. I was drenched in love. My heart was beating so fast it felt like it was bursting out of my chest, like a cartoon character. I stood and stared at all of these people in the park and love exuded from my every pore. I felt blinded by this light and love. And the only thing I knew, in that moment, was that I wanted to work with them, I wanted to serve them. I didn't know how to do that, or why I wanted to do it, or how this would pay my bills, or even how I would start. But I didn't care, I just knew that this is what I had to do.

What I experienced in that moment was unconditional love. I saw the true nature of the people in the park beyond their circumstances. I saw the true nature of me beyond my own insecurities. I saw the true nature of life IS unconditional love. That we are all from the same essence, the same beautiful, pure essence of life and nothing can damage that.

That moment of seeing changed my world completely. I went on to volunteer in the Recovery Community for the next 18 months, helping people uncover their own potential and true nature. I then found myself pitching to work in two prisons in Rugby, one of them for violent men with sexual offences. And starting a social enterprise so that I could share what I had seen with people who were suffering from their own filters which damaged what they are seeing and how they were being in the world.

I realised that it is hurt people who hurt people. They are not born that way. They are hurting others because they are hurt themselves and they continue to hurt others and themselves.

I see that when I lash out it is usually when I'm in pain, anger, insecure, or unhappy. And that is the same for other people.

I've worked with over 500 people at the time of writing and each time I see that when our true nature shows up it always comes with compassion, hope, resilience, love. I see that when I show up in the world with unconditional love my own world is a much nicer place to live.

About Jacqueline Hollows
Jacqueline Hollows is the founder of Beyond Recovery C.I.C (BR), an established social enterprise whose mission is to revolutionise the way addictions and mental health are viewed and treated and to eliminate stigma. Through sharing an understanding of how our experience of life is created from our own minds, the pioneering work that BR does has the potential to reform the criminal justice system from the inside out. The impact on the lives of people BR work with and the results on the broader community have been phenomenal. Jacqueline is also honoured to have been able to share life changing stories and BR's published research from this work, at a number of national and international speaking events. Jacqueline says "I have been working within the criminal justice system (with support professionals and people with convictions) since 2014, delivering our innovative programmes. I have seen that, through a fresh thought in any moment, a deeper level of common sense, wellbeing and resilience is always available regardless to circumstances." Five years on, Jacqueline and her team at BR have established themselves as the thought leaders on this ground breaking work, recognised both in the UK and Internationally.

www.beyond-recovery.co.uk   Twitter @beyond_recovery
LinkedIn   www.linkedin.com/in/jacqueline-hollows-beyond-recovery

Jack Pransky

"All we are is peace, love and wisdom and tho power to create the illusion that we're not."
Jack Pransky

What would you love the world to know about true nature and unconditional love?

When our mind clears, peace, love and wisdom appear. All we have to "do" to see this is look closely at ourselves—see the way it really works within us.

What really does happen within us when our mind clears of all the garbage it carries around? Do we not feel more peaceful in the moment our mind relaxes? Do we not feel more loving of ourselves, of others, and of the earth? Do we not get our best ideas?

Why? Because it is all within us already as part of our "pure consciousness" or soul. We don't have to do anything to try to get it because it is already who we really are!

The only thing blocking us from seeing it is our own personal/egoic thinking. All we have to do is get out of our own way and it will be there for us and everyone else to see.

How has this deeper seeing changed your world?

Before I saw this, I was a seeker of peace, love and wisdom, believing I could only attain it from something outside myself. This led to a whole lot of trying and hard work, and it never really got me anywhere. What a relief to see I didn't have to do anything! Just get out of my own way and observe.

True relief!

About Jack Pransky

I am retired now, after a (fairly) long and fruitful and beautiful life of service to others. Still willing to be of help when asked (if I feel it at the time) but relieved I don't have to be "on" anymore. Now my ten books (so far) can speak for me, or for themselves.

I hope especially Somebody Should Have Told Us!, Seduced by Consciousness, Modello, Hope for All, Parenting from the Heart and my two co-authored children's picture books— What is a Thought (A Thought is A Lot) and What is Wisdom (and Where Do I Find It?—are gifts that keep on giving and continue to provide help to others long after I'm gone.

I can be reached at jack@healthrealize.com

Sara Priestley

"Consciousness is a Love so raw, so powerful, so real, so strong. A Love that knows who I am, without exception or omission. A Love that calls me home on the wild and stormy nights. This Love burns."
from Consciousness, by Sara Priestley

What my heart burns for you to know about unconditional love is this: that you already know. You are complete, here and now.

There is no understanding you need to learn. No course you have to take. Not that there is anything wrong with courses, practices, rituals and learning. But they can't bring you the only thing you ever truly wanted: grace.

Grace is the capacity to navigate life, feeling all of it, deeply, but not suffering. Grace shows up as peace, contentment, happiness, joy, elation, excitement, and sometimes sweet sadness or the cleansing fire of anger. Grace is immersion in the ocean of life, knowing ourselves as the water. Grace shines in the darkness and calls us home. Grace is freedom, and grace is unconditional love.

If this is true, why do you suffer? Why might you feel anxiety, distress, frustration, shame, lack or brokenness? For one reason, and one reason only: that you learnt to believe yourself a tiny, finite wave in the ocean. You were probably taught this, innocently, by your parents, your teachers, your friends and even some spiritual leaders.

But deep down you know, even if just as a faint echo, that you are more than this. You know that grace, freedom and love are possible. The feeling of brokenness sits in dissonance with this echo. It's natural that in feeling broken, you yearn for grace, for freedom, for love. And that you reach to the world for fulfilment.

Notice, each time it seems you've found the answer (or each time you throw in the towel) there's a pause. In that pause, you know grace, you know freedom, you know love. All you ever wanted, seen in the absence of seeking.

This isn't a call to tell the seeking soul to stop. That's near to impossible. Instead, I offer this: consider that this grace—this freedom, this love—is your own true nature. And that it's always apparent in those moments you aren't reaching to the world to fulfil you.

This is what a baby knows instinctively. We're not trying to become like a baby, but it's useful to know that we were born into grace, and that somewhere we lost sight of this knowing.

Fortunately, the knowing never lost sight of us. So, let us turn inward together, back to the heart, back to the essence of life. And, from here, see the world as it truly is. Live it fully. Live as grace, as freedom, as love.

About Sara Priestley
Sara Priestley is a poet, a guide in our exploration of true nature, and mother to four cats. Her first poetry collection, quintessence: the poetry of true nature, is available from Amazon. You can see more of her work at sarapriestley.com.

Judy Nahkies

"If the only thing people learned was not to be afraid of their own experience that alone would change the world."
Syd Banks

Interview

For me true nature/unconditional love is what we are, at our essence, underneath whatever insecure thinking we happen to be listening to in the moment. For most of my life I suffered from anxiety, depression and suicidal thinking. I was incredibly shy, and I had few friends because I was so uncomfortable around people. I would make myself go to social events, on the surface I probably came across as fine but the internal angst was huge and would progressively get worse until I just couldn't stand it any longer and I'd have to go home. I drank a lot too. I said it was because I liked the taste, but I drank because I thought it helped with my social anxiety. I was constantly worried about what I should say or do, and I was so serious. I didn't laugh much, and I suspect I wasn't much fun to be around with my constant low moods making me grumpy and irritable. I think it came from a place of trying too hard, I overthought everything but no matter how hard I tried it seemed I couldn't do better and I felt that I was constantly letting myself down. I used to think "Oh, if only I could put on a better front." I even wondered if I should take acting classes so I could be better at pretending to feel differently than I did, but that felt fake and unauthentic.

At the time I thought I had good reasons for my current depression. Within the space of a year: my mum had passed away of cancer shortly after she was diagnosed; my dad now had cancer and then my daughter had a bad head injury after falling from a horse. We're taught that it's natural to be depressed in those circumstances and I totally bought into that hook, line and sinker. I lost about 12 kgs in weight. I felt sick in every waking moment and I was driving myself crazy with my thinking. I couldn't let my daughter out of my sight, she had depression too and I was so worried.

I was just starting to feel better and getting back riding my horse when an incident made me feel like I'd been stabbed in the back and I was left feeling devastated. It was the proverbial 'straw that broke the camel's back'. All I thought about for weeks was wanting to die. This went on for so long, it got to the point that I was Googling, at 3am one morning, 'how to commit suicide so no one knows you've done it'. I believed that could be my way out of the suffering. I didn't want my family to think I didn't love them enough to stick around but if I could find a way that they didn't have to know, then that would be okay.

I was so lucky that the very next day I stumbled across Michael Neill and the Three Principles and that changed my life. The logic of the Principles just made sense and the overwhelming anxiety fell away almost overnight. When I would start to feel anxious, it often came with the thought 'you must have some anxious thinking' and I ignored it. I was still somewhat bothered by depression/low moods leading to my habitual suicidal thinking. The suicidal thoughts seemed so much more important than other thoughts, but I soon came to see that 'the more comfortable I was being uncomfortable' the quicker I'd feel better. The fact that I was having suicidal thoughts became what Dr Bill Pettit refers to as the 'rumble strip on the side of the road,' a sure sign that I was a bit caught up in a thought storm and to NOT pay attention to my thoughts.

Then one day I had a massive insight where I saw that 'there's never a reason, it's always your thinking.' Although it often doesn't seem like It, we live in the feeling of our thinking not what's going on in the outside world. I started to see how the exact same thing could happen and on one occasion it really bothered me and on another it didn't. Logic says if the circumstance had the power to affect me in a particular way it would work that way ALL the time. It didn't. It totally depended on my mood and whatever I was thinking at the time. Deeply understanding that made a profound difference. I started to use the feeling accompanying my thoughts as a guide as to whether I should take any notice of them. Any thoughts that came with angst were to be ignored, as best as I could. It's still sometimes tempting when I feel bad to 'look for a reason,' thinking that if I can find the reason, I can fix it and change my experience. I forget that the nature of thought is to change without me getting involved and when I do forget I suffer. Other times I see it's better to leave my thinking alone, as best I can, and get on with doing the next obvious thing to do living my life.

I used to be extremely hard on myself, at some level I believed that if I beat myself up enough, I would become the person I wanted to be, but it just kept me stuck. I felt so bad about the thoughts I would have, judging myself harshly because 'I must be really horrible to have THAT thought!' believing I was choosing the random thoughts that popped into my head. I came to see that my thoughts didn't say anything about me as a person, they were simply a consequence of low moods. Ironically, as I became kinder to myself I noticed my mood improved and so too my thoughts.

For most of my life I believed there was something wrong with me. My Doctor told me I'd need to be on medication for the rest of my life. At one stage I was taking 7x the dose of medication that had initially seemed helpful for my anxiety/depression. I tried so many different medications, therapies and self-development programs over the years including psychologists, CBT, NLP, timeline and EFT. I believe that before coming across this simple understanding of how the mind works, I constantly overrode the medication because I was always adding more thinking to thinking. Trying to change my thinking, analysing what was going on, arguing with my suicide thoughts because I thought that stopped me from doing it. Constantly trying to think my way to feeling better, doing better but all that thinking only made things worse.

What I eventually came to see was that underneath all the insecure thinking I already am everything I ever strived to be, confident, creative, compassionate, loving and joyful. I'm not shy at all I just sometimes have some 'shy' thinking! I still do occasionally, but now I just sit quietly and wait for it to pass, there's no need to rush away to change my experience when I know that I'm just one thought away from a completely different experience.

The fake Judy was the person I thought I was, the character I made up based on all the insecure thinking I had. I don't need to work at having all the qualities I wanted, as they are already there, but for my believing thinking that says otherwise.

People that knew me could see it in my face. I often joke that understanding the principles is the best face lift on the planet, that took years off me. I used to have big creases across my forehead and now they're gone. I can see it in my face now if I'm a bit caught up. I can tell by looking in the mirror and I feel it in my body and there's nothing to do. I leave my thinking alone, as best as I can and let the system take care of it.

When I had the insight, 'there's never a reason, it's always your thinking', I was floored at how everything was okay. I honestly thought I was never going to go back to having depression or suicidal thinking again. But it doesn't work that way and that's okay. I don't have depression now; I have low moods for a short time!!

Some big things happened within days of my insight. I had a friend that committed suicide, my daughter had to go to Emergency after another run in with a horse, dad ended up in hospital again. My husband and I were meant to be going away the following week and yet I was in total calm. I had no thinking around it. I knew what to do and I did what needed to be done and I didn't worry about what was going to happen in the future. I took everything in my stride.

Syd Banks' said, 'if the only thing people learned was not to be afraid of their own experience, that alone would change the world,' well that's what happened to me. I'm no longer scared of my experience and it changed my world, it uncovered true nature and unconditional love.

About Judy Nahkies
Judy Nahkies suffered from depression, anxiety and suicidal thinking for decades before stumbling across the Principles in early 2016. Before this simple understanding of how the mind works, Judy lived her life totally at the mercy of her thinking and circumstances. Suddenly life made sense. Judy realised she'd had it all backward, listening to unhelpful thought storms and ignoring quieter wisdom that was trying to point her in a different direction.

The impact was immediate and profound and yet there was more to come. As her understanding deepened, she experienced a level of grace and ease with the ups and downs of life that she couldn't have even imagined previously.

Judy is passionate about sharing what she has learned with individuals and groups, in-person and online. She loves watching clients' stories and labels dissolve, to be replaced by the infinite potential that is inside us all.

Contact Judy at judynahkies@gmail.com

Janet Hill

*"You're only one thought away from happiness, you're only
one thought away from sadness. The secret lies in Thought.
It's the missing link that everybody in the world is looking
for...It's a gift that we were given to have the freedom to walk
through life and see what we want to see. How much better
can it get? That you have the freedom to walk through life
as a free thinker, that is the greatest gift ever, to be a free
thinker."*
Syd Banks

What would you love the world to know about true nature and
unconditional love?

The idea that I can even talk to that question comes as such
a surprise to me. If you had asked me that question, three
years ago, I wouldn't have known what true nature even
meant. Which seems weird to me now. Because how could
you not know what is, in essence, what we're all made of.

If you'd have asked me to talk about unconditional love, I
would have been able to give you examples of love, but they
would have all had conditions attached.

What I'd like to talk about is about how I found love in death.

From the age of 13, I grew up with a brother that had a drug
addiction. It started off as normal, as if drug addiction is even
normal, but by that I mean, he used drugs like a lot of
teenagers and people do. Then his life became for him more
and more complicated, challenging and very difficult.

As a young adult, some of the things that I witnessed were traumatic. The detail doesn't matter as it's irrelevant. With a fresh look know I see amidst all of that trauma there were times when his true nature shone through.

I remember going to visit him in his flat and my heart leapt in a bad way. The flat was everything that you ever imagine in a drug addiction TV show. It was grim. I'd seen it before, seen him in many other horrible situations, but it still shocked me.

We went for a walk along the canal with his dog and I don't remember the detail of the conversation it was just a brother and a sister walking together. The feeling of having my brother with me that day though is what I do remember, in a gorgeous way.

And yes, he was in a mess and his drug addiction was at its worst. Despite that there was a glimpse of his true nature, his kind and sensitive nature.

My brother, Glen, died in October 1999 which as I'm writing this is coming up for 21 years ago. My husband broke the news to me, and I was six months pregnant with our first child. My first thought was, I can't let this impact my baby. And I suppose again, there's that sense of a real sense of inner knowing that I was okay underneath the upset. I wish I had kept looking in that direction over the last 20 years.

Three months after my brother died, my dad died, and my life fell apart or that's how it felt. We had always thought Glen would die young and we lived with that expectation for so many years. It was always a surprise that he had managed to survive up to the age of 34 given the type and number of drugs that he took.

Three years ago, I came across a whole new understanding of state of mind and that we live in the feeling of our thinking and as a result my own experience of anxiety and depression, migraines and strugglo just fell away.

I really understood that the noise in my head was just that and had no meaning. The only thing that had ever been wrong with me was a misunderstanding. Simple.

Nothing actually changed in my life and yet my whole experience of my life was so different, and I saw my own true nature was just hidden by a lot of noise. I saw transformation in others and that everybody has innate mental health.

There was still a big BUT if that's true for everybody and if there is an energy behind life, how the heck did my brother end up dying? Why didn't he wake up to his true nature? There was still annoyance and resistance to seeing everyone's mental health

Then that fell away, and I find myself falling in love with my brother, even though he is dead.

It's hard to see true love when someone is killing themselves.

I really saw and I really sensed that even in death life is just perfect and that we can really never know what death even means and even though writing this is actually bringing tears to my eyes, tears for loss. Yet the tears are peaceful.

His life has so much meaning and yet I can't even tell you what the meaning is. I don't even know. But I know that there is one. It may sound like a strategy of trying to make myself feel better or a rationalisation of his death, but it's just is a sense of knowing.

Glen was a beautiful, beautiful soul who innocently believed the noise in his head and didn't know his own true nature, which is the saddest bit. He innocently found solace in drugs.

The biggest message and the one thing that I would love to share is that everybody, even in death, even in drug addiction has absolute, true mental health.

Waking up to my own true nature has allowed me to be in my own life with more ease and grace and if one person reads this and gets curious then maybe there's the answer to Glen's death. For me now I unconditionally love him and that's just perfect.

Surprisingly, I now find myself as a certified transformational coach and happily combine my existing accountancy career with this new work. Awakening people to their own inner wisdom and the ability to have ease and grace in life was something I never expected to be doing which shows that something knows better than me.

About Janet Hill
I can be reached for a conversation at
janet@janethillcoaching.co.uk.

Phil Goddard

'You must be the change you wish to see in tho world.'
Mahatma Gandhi

The term true nature is often used in spiritual communities as if it's something that can be described or something that you veil, depending upon how you are showing up in the world.

Beyond all our beliefs and opinions of who we think we are and how the world should be there is a timeless and unchanging essence to who we are. This is often described as our true nature or true essence.

I usually refrain from using such terms because they are so easily misunderstood to mean yet another concept, another 'thing' for us to search out and find. Something else to 'be.'

Spiritual teachers have for millennia attempted to describe what this 'true nature' actually is, and I will not attempt to do so here. It is not possible to describe using language since the moment we use words we enter into metaphor and can only describe a concept.

It seems most helpful me to use these terms to point to what it is to be human, whatever that is, without any concepts or ideas, paradoxically, even without the concept of true nature. The 'you' without any ideas of you. The you without any ideas at all, even ideas of God.

We can consider Love in a similar vein. Indeed, perhaps our true nature can be described as Love.

If we recognise that all that we think and describe are ideas that take us beyond what is true, we might consider Love a concept too, and I'll often suggest Love is my favourite idea. Whether we can really know our true nature or know Love is a debate similar in magnitude to whether we can know God, and nations have fought over this for generations.

Perhaps rather than our perpetual search to know, there is freedom in giving up the search and simply allowing life to show us.

Of course, for us to be shown we must be willing to see, and to really see we surely must first start with eyes that are unfiltered and not contaminated by all our conditioned beliefs, ideas and concepts.

Or at least understand that is what is going on, that there will always be beliefs, ideas and concepts and that even when we think we know, we really don't know anything.

And we can surely revel in the joy of that!

Perhaps Joy is our true nature. Perhaps Joy is also Love.

How has this deeper seeing changed your world?

When I reflect on my twenty-two years exploring human behaviour and the nature of our human experience, one elemental understanding above all else dominates the transformations that have taken place in my life as a result of this exploration.
All love is unconditional. If it has conditions, it's not love.

The most profound change in my life that is a reflection of this understanding is the transformation of my relationship with my dad. I used to think my dad, despite being a dedicated provider for his family, didn't deserve my love and respect. He'd done many things that as a parent I'd never dream of doing, some of which would be considered abusive.

He'd said things that, on reflection, shocked me that a dad would say such things to his son or daughter. He'd treated his first wife, my dear mum, in a way that I thought no man should ever treat a woman.

In so many ways I thought he should have behaved very differently.
And the truth is, even now, I'd prefer that he did.
And yet…

What I've seen, to varying degrees at different times, deeper as time and my understanding has evolved, is…

I've done many things as a parent I wish I'd not done, some of which now, in the 21st century, would also be considered abusive. I've said many things that, on reflection, I wish I'd never said. I've certainly treated people in ways I don't think anyone should be treated, irrespective of whatever they might have done.

And I know I loved my family with all my heart. I clung on to the idea of us all being together for way longer than was good for any of us, to the detriment of all of us.

I can see that I could not have behaved differently given the understanding I had at the time. And none of that was any direct representation of the huge huge love I have in my heart for my family.

Indeed, the dynamics of the relationships in that family are not even a great representation of the love in my heart today. There is still work that could be done.

My dad learnt parenting from the draconian ideas of his own father. I was just fortunate that, eventually anyway, something inside of me had me step out of those ideas.

Moments of good fortune.

I'm very compassionate to the young man that became a stepdad overnight at the age of twenty. I had no idea what the hell I was doing, and it was a very, very tough journey with very little encouragement, a lot of complex pressures, and I failed miserably in many respects.

In other ways I did pretty amazing.

And I loved relentlessly under some excruciatingly difficult circumstances.

I spent most of adult life wishing my dad was different. Wishing I'd had a different dad. Wishing for something that simply was not possible. What a sneaky way to torture myself and convince myself it was him continuing to be doing the torturing…

Fortunately for us both, a time arrived when I got to see past my own judgments, my own egotistic and dispassionate ideas of how my dad 'should be', and let his love in.

A moment arrived when I saw the extent of my own stories that kept me from seeing the true nature of him.

I have immense compassion for him. He was certainly doing his best, faced some tough decisions, particularly when he was living with his second wife, and I know on reflection he'd make different choices now. He's missed out on soooo much.

Lifetimes, grandchildren growing up, weddings. He's already paid a very heavy price for not living up to our 'standards.'

But the fact that hc loves all his children is in no doubt. When I go see him now, he lights up with absolute glee. It's like he can't contain his love, and I'm often a little embarrassed at just how pleased he is.

It's only me, Dad…

He's still very opinionated… and he knows that too, recognising that he doesn't need to be taken seriously anymore and he probably doesn't have much time left.

A couple of years ago we hugged, probably for the first time in forty years, and when we meet we sit on the same sofa.

I'm happier than I've ever been that he's still around, and neither of us are clinging on to ideas that deny us a more loving experience of each other.

Love is always available. It's much easier to see that when we let go of our own ideas of judgement and victimhood. It's much easier to see that with understanding and compassion. It's much easier to feel love when we stop holding up our own ideas against others.

About Phil Goddard
Phil Goddard helps business owners and leaders enjoy their personal relationships as much as they enjoy their work, creating easy, prosperous and loving personal & professional relationships. He is an internationally renowned life & relationship coach, speaker, leadership consultant, and lover of life and humanity. A published author, he is also the host of both The Coaching Life and Naked Hearts Podcasts. His

work centres around transforming relationships and leadership through developing a deeply grounded understanding of the principles behind our human experience and the nature of how our experience of life is created.

With humour and sincerity, he combines over twenty-one years in corporate leadership with fifteen years as a professional coach, to help organisations build harmonious and highly productive teams, and individuals to live their most loving and joyous lives.

He has coached Hollywood actors, international models, journalists, artists, authors, film directors, corporate executives, and numerous business owners, leaders and entrepreneurs. He is a digital nomad and can often be found on the Greek Island of Zakynthos, where he holds exclusive coaching immersion retreats for individual clients.

He challenges his work on happiness by following a few English sports teams.

Phil can be contacted via philg.com and found on Facebook via fbphil.com

Elizabeth Scott

"The meaning of life is just to be alive. It is so plain and so obvious and so simple. And yet, everybody rushes around in a great panic as if it were necessary to achieve something beyond themselves."
Alan W. Watts, The Culture of Counter-Culture: Edited Transcripts

When I look in the mirror, I see my face staring back. Imperceptibly it changes daily; but the change is so gradual that I only realise the difference when I look at old photos.

In my old photos I see youth, blooming skin and dark shiny hair. Now there are wrinkles and a lot of grey. Back then I had fierce views about work, about justice, about finding my purpose and proving my worth. Nowadays as I look in the mirror, I know I have mellowed. I love nature, I write, and I am happiest walking and taking my time.

The question I ask most frequently now is: 'Who am I?'

I am not my body – because that has altered and aged. I am not my views because they are markedly different and still transform to this day. I am not my personality – that too has morphed.

Can you see how tricky it is to answer the question: 'Who am I?' The person I see in the mirror (both physical and psychological) never stays the same – that person has been constantly mutating (and still is). There is so much that is transient and temporary about that 'mirror' person; so: Who am I? What is the thread of consistency that is at the centre of my being?

It's only in recent years that I've come to realise that looking for myself in the face that stares back from the mirror is the wrong place to look. Looking for myself amidst the ideas, beliefs and personality traits I exhibit is not where the true me exists. I wish I'd known years earlier where to look for the answer to the question: "Who am I?"

Our true essence and core are much more than our bones, skin and flesh. Our true nature is much more than the erratic, every shifting thoughts, beliefs and feelings. If you want to see your true nature you will never find it in the person staring back from the mirror.

Where is your true nature? When you look within to the space of stillness, peace and love – you are looking in the right direction. Your true nature is the ever-present awareness and sense of knowing. When you start your exploration here you begin to see the connection of love, compassion and kindness that is the common thread uniting us all.

The face looking back at you in the mirror is just a mask – look beyond the mask.

How has this deeper seeing changed your world?

What would it be like if you could set sail in an unsinkable boat? What if you knew that regardless of the weather and sea conditions - whether it was hurricanes or giant waves – that your boat was unsinkable?

You would still sometimes feel scared and you would still feel sad – but one thing you would also know (however scared or insecure you felt) was that your boat could not sink.

It is like having a constant life-raft in the stormy seas of life.

When I feel overwhelmed and sad or when I feel unloved and unworthy – that is when the seas of life feel frightening and threatening However, this life-raft of 'knowing' – this sense of my true essence and the deeper intelligence behind life, has been my go-to space.

It doesn't guarantee an easy life it doesn't guarantee success or fortune – but the life-raft guarantees that whatever adventures I might engage in – I will ultimately be safe at the deepest level of my being.

About Elizabeth Scott
My work involves sharing a hopeful message of mental wellbeing in communities, schools and businesses. We run a social enterprise called *Inner Compass Guide CIC*. The Wellbeing Listener project is our most popular programme; it is a simple way of people looking within for their constant resourcefulness, resilience and clarity. We believe everyone has a right to be heard at the level of soul. www.innercompassguide.com

Andrea Morrison

"You are the sun, even on a cloudy day you shine just as brightly
even though it might not feel like that."
Andrea Morrison

Interview

What would you love the world to know about true nature and unconditional love?

That we are that. We already are unconditional love; we have everything we need. I think we get so innocently caught up with what we think our true nature is, when the truth is that what we believe are simply ideas that we have about ourselves. For example we may believe that our true nature is that we are 'not good with people' or that we're not confident or competent in some way, we have all these beliefs, based upon our experience and we wrap all of those loose ideas up and we believe that that's our true nature, who we really are.

What I would love others to see is that our true nature is way beyond all those ideas, it is so much purer and in that purity is everything that we are seeking, but we so often don't see it for what it is. It's so funny that when we catch a glimpse of our true nature, we so often dismiss it as a nice feeling, maybe we think it's not real life or the real us because of the ideas and beliefs that we have. But in that moment, what we are experiencing is our true nature really shining through, full of love, kindness, understanding, hope, joy and ease.

I remember when my kids were small and life felt so chaotic and stressful to me, but there were moments when I'd just be watching them play, being so full of life and joyful, and my heart would just overflow with love. In that moment, I was so present with them, I wasn't thinking about what I had to do, or whoro I had to be, or engaged with any of the thousands of stressful or insecure thoughts. It was such a beautiful feeling, and in that moment, I had everything I needed, everything I was searching for. Life felt rich and beautiful. Although those moments were fleeting, I recognise now that those moments were when I was resting in my true nature.

When we catch a glimpse of our true nature, we really feel that unconditional love, the love that has no limitations, the love that life has for us – we are literally experiencing the universal life force that runs through every human being, a deeper intelligence that is available to all of us.

When we fall back into that loving space, we are far more understanding and compassionate towards ourselves and our humanness. The knock on effect of this is when we see it for ourselves, we start to appreciate more that this is true for every human being, everyone's true nature is beautiful and perfect, it's the nature of the universal force that runs through them too. It may be seemingly buried under layers of insecure thinking, or fear, or stress, but it is still there. We can see that our true nature has to be unbreakable, it's as good as new as the day we were born and that it has everything we seek, happiness, joy, kindness, love, understanding. That is who we all are innately.

Even when we see behaviours in ourselves or from others that we might not like, knowing who we are innately, what runs through us, enables us to understand that the behaviour isn't who we are and it transforms the relationship we have with it. There is a knowing that in that moment that we (or they) are simply and innocently lost in thought, which is part of being human after all. With this understanding brings a kindness and a love, that behaviour isn't the person, it's transient. It's not who we are. It is so beautiful.

How has this deeper seeing changed your world?

I came from such a place of chaos, stress, worry, fear, doubt, lack of confidence and negative thinking. It was a world that seemed to me to be hard and tough and I did not understand it. I was really stressed, I was coming out of burnout and desperately trying to recover. It was always like Groundhog Day with a perpetual rollercoaster included for free. It did not matter what I did on the outside, I just continually felt this suffering.

When I came across this understanding, I was very resistant to begin with. I thought that I was way too complicated and way too broken for anything to help me. I wanted a magic pill or a magic solution, or a strategy to help me cope with my brokenness. However, this understanding enabled me to see that I was so much more than the ideas I had about myself and those around me. It enabled me to see the nature of literally what I was rooted in, the source of my experience and what I had going for me.

The more I saw about our true nature, the more I saw how this deeper intelligence is such a rich resource that is available to us, but even though it was there I had never recognised it so life always looked really scary. I always felt like everything was on me to figure out, how I could get it wrong because I didn't know enough, I didn't have enough experience, I simply wasn't enough. I began to see how this deeper intelligence is available to all of us to draw on, that when I look in that direction and try to 'figure it out' less in my head, life unfolds naturally. Life whilst unknown has a deeper certainty about it because I know no matter what the future holds, I have this deeper resource available to me.

I found that as I began to see this, the relationship that I had with the layers and layers of thinking that I had been doing started to change. For the most part I paid less attention to it, it wasn't that it disappeared, often it was still there, but it didn't impact me as much, it made less sense to take it into account when I lived my life. However, the times that I did get sucked into my thinking, which is the nature of our human experience, I found I was far more compassionate and understanding, when the moment passed, I thought less and less about it. I saw deeply that I didn't need to fix these moments, I didn't need to avoid them, or prevent them, they would pass, and when they did, they stayed in the past.

The consequence of seeing this is that all aspects of my life are so much more straightforward, life has an ease to it now and is so joyful, there is a lightness about it.

About Andrea Morrison
At the moment I'm enjoying coaching and mentoring in this understanding, it's such a beautiful thing to share and witness the impact that it has in other's lives. What I'm also loving is watching how my practice is unfolding for me and I'm just seeing more and more how it's not on me to 'create' it as much as I previous thought I was. Before I would be a planner and a goal setter, I would really try to 'make' things happen, I lived in a state of not wanting to get it wrong, and if I made the wrong decision I could be missing out! Whilst I created a business that way, it was so hard!

There wasn't a freshness about what I was doing, and I can see now that a large part of what I created was rehashed ideas and old thoughts, other people's or my own strategies and ideas! What I love now is really seeing how our deeper intelligence enables us to experience fresh thinking, for ideas literally popping in our heads, how we can create something fresh and new. I love running with them! I love watching this unfold.

But moreso I love how I know it's not on me, on my personal intellect, to work my business out. I used to want to know what I was doing next week, next month, in a year's time. Knowing that my security doesn't rest there is empowering. That all I need to know is my next step, that the universal intelligence has the future covered, I don't need to work that out. It has enabled me to see that I really can't fail at this, that there is no right way, no best way, no rigid definition of success, that I have to work out how to achieve. If I get caught up in my thinking, if I don't listen to what I know it makes no difference to the outcome, I keep moving, and the universal intelligence is there with me every step of the way.

www.andreamorrison.co.uk

Nicole Barton

"We are born of love; Love is our Mothor."
Rumi

Despite so much apparent 'difference' and conflict in the world these days, I have come to rediscover that underneath all of our ideas about separation, we are all the same. Any feelings of love being lacking are just ideas. For much of my life I felt that I was alone, that I was unlovable and that I was separate – due to a lot of thinking about the day that my dad left my life at age 4, on my first day of school, never really to return. This led me to create what I now like to describe as 'stories' that I was 'not enough'. For much of my life, from this space, I felt broken, and I would respond to the world as if I wasn't good enough and needed fixing. Until one day, I came across an understanding which pointed towards our true nature. By this, I mean I rediscovered who we 'really are' – beyond our narratives and ideas – and that is that our essence is love.

Who we were born as was love, and what lies beyond all 'story' is love. I realised in this that we can't ever not be 'enough,' and it changed everything. In nature, I began to see that there was a beautiful wisdom to life when it was left alone. That the same thing that grows the trees beats our hearts and allows us to breathe; no 'doing' involved. Trees don't worry about whether their leaves will fall off in Autumn, just as they don't worry about being 'enough' – and we are just the same. This realisation is so profound because this is who we all are. In seeing this, we realise that 'love' and 'conditions' are just concepts of the mind, for who we are is magic, in action – some might call it unconditional love. And it's within us all; it's what we are born of.

Seeing this deeper dropped me out of a need for comparison, seeking anything to 'fix' me, out of a need to look externally from myself for love. In fact, it stopped me from even thinking of myself as unlovable. I used to think that love was conditional on me 'being' a certain way – being successful, joyful, lovable – but all of this fell away as I leant deeper into exploring who we really are beyond all of these ideas. And the good thing is, that as I saw this more, and saw the nature of how we 'think' – the fact that we make up our realities – and that underneath that made up story of who we are is this beautiful wisdom to life, I began to settle out of all of the thinking and behaviours that kept me feeling stuck. In the space where once had been anxiety, fear and keeping myself small, I began to unravel into a feeling of peace, wholeness, creativity and expansion – as well as acceptance and presence.

Now, I see that life is living as me; that we are all love at our true essence, and that anything else is a misunderstanding. Life is softer; gentler, somehow. Life is lived with greater love and understanding, and a feeling of connection – because we can't be separate from love. We are love. And that is a profoundly special, freeing and life-changing realisation. And contained within that is the capacity for us to embrace the gift of thought to instead unravel a beautiful life we love, filled with creative desire! Life is a gift, and its enjoyment is all born of the simply understanding that we are love.

About Nicole Barton
Life Mentor, Coach, Speaker and Writer, Nicole Barton, is something of a unicorn within the self-help industry for her candid notion that nobody needs self-help. She is a breath of fresh air in her admission that while playing in anything that leads us into 'soul-led expression' is beautiful to shift us from

our heads and into our hearts, none of these practices are prerequisites to peace, joy or creativity.

Nicole supports creatives to embody their own wisdom and unravel a life they love, through embracing powerful self-rediscovery. She does this via her online summit, Self-Rediscovery School group programs, one-to-ones, events and retreats, and is working on her first book. Visit her at www.nicolebarton.co.uk.

Instagram - www.instagram.com/wellbeingwriter
Facebook - www.facebook.com/TheWellbeingWriter
Website - www.nicolebarton.co.uk

Lana Bastianutti

"The mind creates the abyss, the heart crosses it."
Sri Nisargadatta Maharaj

Love is Who We Are

Tina Turner, the American singer-songwriter once famously asked, "What's Love got to do with it?" Would you believe me if I said, "Everything."?

It doesn't take much to see the truth in this. Ask any person lying upon their deathbed to reveal what is most important in life and they will confess that it is Love. Always Love. The clarity with which they see this simple truth is singular in its focus. And yet, we, as the living, often overlook this heartfelt realization or perhaps, more importantly, misunderstand the profound truth of it as it relates to our own lives.

While most people think of love as a sensation that we feel in response to the outside world, I would suggest that Love - unconditional Love - is who we are at our core. It is our default setting and synonymous with our true nature. And when we fall open to this nature, we find that unconditional Love is as effortless as it is life changing.

Beyond the words of the dying let's also look to the opposite end of the lifeline for insight into our fundamental nature. Very young children, after all, are the closest manifestation of this nature in form. When not hungry, tired or soiled, small children fall open to this natural state of unconditional Love. Watch any young child and you will instantly be transported into their world where fireflies are magical, muddy puddles are an invitation for fun, and any living creature becomes an instant best friend. In the eyes of a child, all of life is met with an unconditional loving presence devoid of judgment. And it is in this state of unconditional Love that we humans thrive.

One of the most profound examples of this came from a story I heard about a man who called a Suicide Hotline and declared that he planned to take his own life that night. Before doing so, however, he wanted to talk to someone. He insisted that whoever he talked to must NOT make any attempts to change his mind and that if they did, he would hang up the phone and proceed with his plan. The person who took the call that night assured the man that he would respect his wishes. And so, the two began to converse; each taking turns as they talked and then listened. By all accounts, it seemed like a normal conversation between two individuals. When the man at the hotline center finally hung up the phone, his colleagues asked after the welfare of the caller. The man replied that the caller had assured him that he was feeling much better and realized that he no longer wanted to take his own life. When asked what he'd done to create this turnaround, the man replied, "I simply loved him."

What this story demonstrates is the truly transformative power of unconditional Love - free from need or expectation or judgment.
In fact, coming from a place of pure love, one human soul was able to reach another human soul who was suffering, so that they, in turn, were able to reconnect with their own true nature and love for Life itself.

So, if unconditional Love is our true nature and we thrive in such a state, what gets in the way of living from that place?

The answer lies in understanding how our experience is created.

In truth, our personal realities are brought to life via the formless energy of Thought which we experience in form through our moment to moment thinking and feeling. Our behaviors then flow from that thinking and feeling. This trifecta of thought, feeling, and behavior is commonly known as our psychology. So when we wonder what gets in the way of our true nature, the simple answer is - our psychology. When we engage and identify exclusively with our psychology we become less present, aware, and grounded in our true nature.

So, let's imagine, if you will, the first blush of love. Recall that at the beginning of a relationship, we are consumed by an open unconditional loving feeling for our partner. We are, in effect, completely aligned with our true nature of unconditional Love. In fact, any experience that doesn't support a loving feeling is summarily rejected, ignored, or transformed by this alignment; that snorty little laugh is met with loving adoration rather than annoyance; the incessant cleanliness is met with fascination and acceptance rather than judgment, and that habit of nervous throat clearing is met with profound compassion rather than contempt.

In this natural state of unconditional Love, we become engaged, committed, and present to the health and success of our relationship and in so doing create an environment in which our relationship can thrive since inherent within unconditional Love lie qualities such as connection, compassion, humor, and acceptance.

So what happens to this unconditional Love?
As time goes by, we tend to get a tad bit comfortable and a lot more unconsciously engaged and caught up in our thinking! Our initial singular focus and presence become more muted as our minds begin to engage in other things and other thinking. As such, we tend to forget about "showing up" consciously in our Loving presence and instead lean on old

habits of being, learnings, and deep-seated beliefs that developed in our formative years.

Over time we find ourselves reacting in ways that may seem automatic and familiar but are far from our alignment to our true nature. In our minds, the snorty laugh that was once adorable becomes obnoxious, the incessant cleanliness becomes suffocating, and the nervous throat-clearing becomes disdainful. These new reactions to familiar experiences do not arise from our innate nature of unconditional Love but rather from a personal mind that can't help but narrate, evaluate, and judge our lives.

In fact, if we look closely at these reactions we find that they more often than not echo and mirror the words and behaviors of our parents, or caregivers, or community, or culture. In other words, we innocently imitate and adopt the learned psychology of others. In doing so, we, and our relationships, can suffer, particularly when we identify more with that psychology than with our true nature.

Our innocent covering over of our nature and misidentification with our psychology reminds me of the story of the Golden Buddha. Back in 1957, a group of Thai monks were moving a giant clay Buddha. As they did so, one of the monks noticed a crack in the clay from which emanated a strange golden light. Curious, the monk began to chip away at the clay until he soon discovered that the statue was made of solid gold. Historians now believe that hundreds of years earlier, Thai monks had purposely covered the Buddha in clay in an attempt to protect it from an invading army. And while the statue was preserved, its true golden nature lay forgotten for centuries.

So how do we uncover our own Golden Buddha?

We trust - secure in the knowledge that unconditional Love lies just beneath the surface of our thinking. It IS who we are when we aren't busy staring at our psychology and listening to our personal mind. What we inevitably find is as our thinking begins to crack and break away, our true nature of unconditional Love shines through.

And that is everything.

About Lana Bastianutti
Lana is a Life Coach and her website is Lanabcoaching.com

Jason Shiers

"All you have to do is realize that it's Thought. The second you realize that it's Thought, you are touching the very essence of psychological experience. You're back to the "now," you're back to happiness.
Syd Banks"

What would you love the world to know about true nature and unconditional love?

Regardless of how broken you feel, how damaged you think you are, how many or how few struggles you have felt during your life time, how many mental health diagnoses you have received or what crimes you have committed, there is a place in you that is untouchable, unbreakable, always okay, that place in you that knows when something is off, when something is not right, that place in you that has pointed you here to reading this, that place in you that recognises the deeper truth when it is spoken, even if the intellect is not following.

Love is not a place to get to, love is who we are, when we are not making up stories about ourselves, it's a place to come from. It is a feeling that is inside all of us, at all times, that is accessible everywhere and anywhere. Somewhere that words cannot describe but can be felt.

When you rest in the now, when you become present to this moment, right here, right now, where nothing else matters, everything is always okay, only we can take ourselves away from that.

Find a person who sees that in you, and can help you find it in yourself, because it's life changing and it's permanent.

How has this deeper seeing changed your world?

Coming from a place of endless daily suffering, a life filled with depression, anxiety, misery and constant addiction with no hope. To living the life of my dreams without changing my outside world or external circumstances.

It always looked to me that unless I had a drastic good fortune, that one day someone pulled up with a 'this is your life' book or bag of money that I would be suffering forever. Even after the life of drugs and crime was over, and I was being a 'productive' member of society, I was still suffering in my internal world, it's strange how I thought that's okay though, as long as I don't take medication to escape, then it's better than how it was.

Life had got drastically better on the outside, I had got a job, I paid bills I even had friends, and my family no longer called the police when I visited. On the inside though was a whole different story, I was fearful of what I had escaped from for all these years, the tragic loss of my dad in an accident as a small boy. It looked that I would somehow have to face the feelings I had been dodging my whole life. So, I continued to escape in whatever I could, as long as it wasn't drugs. Whatever made me feel better, I did more of it, where I pretty much identified with any 12-step fellowship going.

I lived a life of suffering, thinking I was hopeless and there was no way out, after trying every therapy I could find, doing all the processes, meditations, training as a psychotherapist, training in person centred therapy and in NLP, doing the Hoffman Process and Tony Robbins Mastery University. A chance encounter with the work of Michael Neill sent me in a new direction.

In a momentary realisation, I saw the truth of who I was, and how I had created my own misery over all the years and then tried to escape from it in every possible way. I was not who I thought I was, and no-one else thought of me the way I thought they did, nor did I have to achieve, gain status, get more money to be who I thought I needed to be to be okay. My whole world was made of thought, and the walls had just fallen. I had a sense of knowing that life had changed, but I couldn't make complete sense of it, words just don't do justice to trying to understand the unexplainable. Insight – a sight from inside, the seeing of what is true for us already, a seeing that is life changing, that gives us a different perspective, and allows life as we know it be different without a change in circumstances.

About Jason Shiers
As well as coaching @ Wide World Coaching, I have been having transformative conversations with people over @ www.misunderstandingsofthemind.com about all different areas of life, that my clients seem to love and find helpful.

www.infiniterecovery.co.uk is my new addiction treatment programme going live in 2020 to help treat addiction through a 3 Principles understanding.

Rita J Shuford, Ph.D.

"When the answers are complicated, it's the Intellect.
When the answers are simple, it's the Spirit."
Syd Banks

Interview

What would you love the world to know about true nature and unconditional love?

That it's who we are. Unconditional love is who we are at the core. That is a spiritual truth. It's the essence of all life. Thus, there's nothing to fear. Peace of mind is unconditional. The spiritual intelligence of all life is the essence of our soul.

There's no way we cannot be that spiritual essence every minute of our life. We can only believe that we're something other than that, which is the normal thing for human beings to begin to believe in one way or another. Our illusionary beliefs can never change the fact that who and what we are is 'God'. This 'God' intelligence is the spiritual essence of all things whether in form or formless. It is not religious in nature and yet all religions stem from and point to this divine power. The beauty is that "we are what we seek." Unconditional love and understanding, purity of mind, thought and consciousness, is the core of our being.

In any moment our minds are clear and present, secure and free to see what is without fear or judgement. In another moment we have lost our inside out perspective via our innocent misuse of the gift of thought, this incredible power to think, to have thought and see life always from within our own mind and thought. Waking up to the inside out spiritual nature of our experience is our birthright. Even though, in the moment, it may appear otherwise, we are never more than a thought away from the truth of who and what we are...spiritual beings. It's a beautiful thing the truth.

The 3 Principles are the creative power bridge that help us understand how, nothing, formless energy, the spiritual energy of all things becomes something, the physical reality we see and live in and the personal experiences we are having moment to moment. We are always seeing life from within our own mind and thought, knowingly or not. As we begin to realize that our experience really is coming from within and it really is a divine thought experience we are having from moment to moment, that realization starts to shift the way we are thinking naturally. Our mind will not hang on to what it realizes isn't true.

The shifts happen in moments. We get all caught up and upset about something and talk to ten people and they all agree with us. Something or someone in our life is causing our upset. Yet, the inner struggle and stressful feelings, the mental story we're in, really is the product of our own mind and thought at the time. To say this is not to be in denial of anything. There's lots of stuff going on in life, sometimes more problematic than at other times. As Sydney Banks said denial would be stupid. I'm paraphrasing but to deny is not what this is about, it's to see what is from wisdom, a perspective of understanding where our experience is coming from now, in the moment, in the now, from within, which is all we really have. When we see the inside out source of our stress, struggle and upset our mind naturally calms and clears, opening the door for wisdom and commonsense.

How has this deeper seeing changed your world?

It keeps changing my world. Which is something that I've always loved about finding a deeper truth. It's a never-ending revelation going on. Initially, for me, it was knowing I had found what I was looking for, the core truth, the missing link. I knew it in my heart and soul the first time I heard Syd speak on tape. It's been 40 some years now and I keep learning and growing. Waking up is timeless, truth is timeless and eternal. It's outside of time, space, and matter.

I would say, in just the last few years, I've had some of the deepest insights. What that's done for me personally, is that I just live with a quieter mind more of the time. I'm more at ease. My mind is more open to the moment, which is how we come into life. An infant, a child, they're just open, they don't have any judgment or fear. That is a learned way of thinking, not right or wrong, it's normal. The idea that there's an outside-in determiner for human experience is the biggest misunderstanding that perpetuates human suffering in life. For me, the beliefs that I have that have carried that misunderstanding have fallen away more. This leaves the aperture of my mind, wider, more open and that aperture is a channel for more pure love and understanding for myself and others. I have less judgement and more recognition of when I've lost my alignment with truth.

When I lose my alignment with the truth, when I forget where my experience is coming from, it looks like it's that person across the street, that's why I'm angry. It doesn't mean they are not being difficult, but that's really about where they are at, not who they are. I think that's the big, big thing. It's really seeing beyond the personal filters that people are living in and from to the truth of it, of who and what that person is. I was just talking to somebody yesterday about this who was in the military for quite a while and was taught to be a tough guy. He is just starting to realize that's a role he took on and has lived for over 20 years. Deep down, he's just got this incredible, beautiful feeling for people. He's in a transition is what I'm hearing and seeing. It's like finding our way home to who and what we really are.

Our home within is where we've always been in truth. We cannot be in life without this soul consciousness giving us life. To begin to even question the role that we've been playing, in this case, as the tough guy, is a step within, an openness to seeing who and what we really are. What a relief it is when we see that we each have those ideas about ourselves, in our own way, an image we need to portray and maintain. Some of us need to be a little more tough guy sometimes, there's not a right or wrong here. It's just finding our true self, which is not a personal self. It is a spiritual identity that is the essence of who and what we all are. It is a universal identity. It is the logic and wisdom of our soul and it's within each of us that we find it.

Finding and listening to that Inner truth and guide, more and more, is to trust our own wisdom and common sense. Recognizing, by the way I'm feeling, that I'm probably not operating in the moment from clarity and wisdom, quiets our mind, creating an inner space to take a different look at what is going on inside and out. It simplifies what's going on from within our own minds. I've always preferred simple, simple common sense.

The 3 principles help us understand more insightfully that it is our use of the power of thought, in the moment, determining how we feel, inside out. If the way I am thinking/feeling is getting in the way of clarity and well-being, 'seeing' that it is thought, sets in motion a natural, built in, spiritual mind treatment of letting go, letting pass the temporary unhelpful way I am thinking. We are no longer stuck in blame, judgement, worry, stress, over analysis, etc.

Recognizing thought in motion helps clear away what has innocently gotten in the way, some belief/misunderstanding that our feelings and reactions can be caused or determined by something other than our own mind and thought in the moment. Circumstances, events, conditions, other peoples' behavior and reactions exist but do not hold the power to determine how we feel and react.

Change is natural, it's like the shedding of old leaves so new ones can grow. Like I said to this fellow yesterday, "there is a part of you that is seeing that the 'tough guy' is just something you learned and not who you are or want to be all the time. You are already changing from within."

We're built for new; we're built for now and we have the wisdom and commonsense we need for now. Sometimes that wisdom is that we don't know the answer right now. That puts us back into the unknown, the unknown is spiritual. When I realized that the unknown was spiritual, I stopped struggling so much trying to figure out stuff and let my mind rest knowing the clarity and answers would come.

Back to your question, how has deeper understanding changed my world. I'm living with less unnecessary thought on my mind, more and more peace of mind and more neutrality and compassion. I always had a certain amount of compassion, but I had to learn compassion for myself. I was more self-critical, now the frequency is less, the intensity is less. I still forget true nature, but then I wake up and remember. Once you start waking up to that fact, you can't stop that evolution in yourself.

We can get plateaued; I've certainly been plateaued because I believed something that wasn't true about me or my life. Then in a moment the truth starts to reveal itself that it's some insecurity, which is always thought. There is no other way we can have insecurity except to have an insecure thought. It's a powerful truth and a lovely way of life that comes out of that truth. I feel like I'm always beginning, always having a second chance to see and experience life anew, to enjoy life more, to live with more gratitude, ease and wellbeing, going with the flow, no matter what.

What are you up to in the world?

This is my calling to be in service to truth, in whatever way that shows up. What I do varies, I'm doing coaching, mentoring, and counseling by zoom, phone and in person. This month I'm starting a new project a monthly group entitled, "Begin Within: A 3 principles Deep Dive Group." In the local community there is a new project coming on board that I'm probably going to get involved with. It's a residential program that's being developed for sex trafficked girls. What I'm hearing in terms of their program and treatment philosophy, is one that I think I could really get behind. They see the health in these girls and are looking to really draw that out of them.

About Dr. Rita Shuford
Dr. Shuford is a licensed psychologist and Certified Practitioner of the Three principles. She met Sydney Banks in 1977. For 40+ years Dr. Shuford has been a student and teacher of the Three principles. She has worked in a variety of settings including schools, hospitals and community and private mental health clinics. Dr. Shuford has been Director of Clinical Services in three clinics in Florida and Hawaii. She has mentored, provided training, and supervised many colleagues and fellow students of the Three Principles. She is the Founder and CEO of Three Principles Hawaii.
www.threeprincipleshawaii.com

Billy Mann

"The gardener smiled, heaved an enormous, dramatic sigh, and then repeated the words, simplicity, simplicity, simplicity. Why is simplicity so complicated?"
Syd Banks - Enlightened Gardener Revisited

A Letter Of Unconditional Love To Me

Dear Me,

It's been a long while since we last got together. I wanted to let you know that I'm here for you always.

I've watched over you struggle for so many years.

I've watched over you even though you felt so alone as if nobody in the world even knew you existed.

I've watched over you as you've looked away from me looking for an answer that you were told you needed.

I've watched over you as you searched for that answer, over and over.

I've watched over you as you got hurt over and over.

I've watched over you when the pain broke your heart into a thousand pieces.

I've watched over as you prayed, looking for that guidance.

I've watched over you as you thought that you didn't deserve all the good life has to offer.

I've watched over you as you thought you were so different that nobody would understand you.

I watched over you as you got angry and frustrated with the world that doesn't seem to understand you.

I've watched over you as you thought there was no point going on.

I've watched over you even when you forgot about me.

And now I want you to hear me speak.

I LOVE YOU UNCONDITIONALLY.

Do you know what that means?

I love you so much that all that stuff you think doesn't actually matter.

I love you so much that it doesn't matter who you think you are, I know you.

I love so much that when your heart is breaking, I'm silently holding you deeply so you can heal.

I love you so much because you are already beautiful.

I love you so much because I get you as you truly are.

I love you so much because you're so special as you are.

I love you so much that I want you to have all of life's joy.

I love you so much that I love you unconditionally.

I love you even when you think I don't.

I love your odd socks of ideas.

I love your big loud laugh at the wrong time.

I love your quiet tears when you think nobody's looking.

I love your moments of awkwardness.

I love your shyness.

I love your gentleness.

I love your decency.

I love your kindness.

I love your art.

I love your passion when you're fired up about injustice.

I love how you're not the same as everyone else.

I love how your heart sings.

I love how you love.

I love all the bits of you.

I Love you unconditionally.

I Love you.

I am You.

We Are.

Unconditional.

Love.

About Billy Mann
You can find Billy on Facebook & Instagram @ Billy Mann Coaching and you can contact him @ billymanncoaching@gmail.com

Christopher Mavinga

"Life is like any other contact sport; you're gonna get your knocks. But it's not the knocks that count, it's how you handle them. If you handle them with anger, distrust, jealousy, hate, this in return is what you're going to get. But if you handle these knocks with love and understanding, they don't mean much. They just dissipate."
Sydney Banks

Interview

What would you love the world to know about true nature and unconditional love?

I'd like the world to know that true nature is everywhere. It's everywhere!

If you take your time and you're present, you don't need to look, you can just feel that there is love everywhere. Love is everywhere you go. Literally!

Sometimes you find love in the strangest places, I came across it in prison. At that time, it was not love I was expecting to find. But I found unconditional love when the Beyond Recovery team saw something in me, a spark. They actually listened to me and allowed me to express myself. I was experiencing a lot of shameful feelings about my past and the things I'd done. But the experience got me to love. I was able to unpeel myself and reveal to myself and the world who I really am.

In Beyond Recovery I found a community. I felt wanted and I felt that self-power again, it was like when a flower hasn't been nurtured for so long but once you start nurturing it, it starts to blossom again. And that's the only way I can describe my experience of uncovering true nature and unconditional love.

Before Beyond Recovery I was tied up in my old ways of thinking. I wasn't taking care of my own wellbeing. I was thinking far ahead into the future when I hadn't even dealt with today's situation. My new understanding got me back into now. In a strange way it's given me some vital seconds that I didn't think I had before. It has changed my world for the better. I've got compassion now and awareness. I've got those vital seconds to think clearly before I act.

A prime example is, I used to get into my head when I was in prison when my girlfriend didn't answer the phone. Once I'd got this understanding, when she didn't answer the phone, I didn't go so quick, making up stories about what she was doing. It helped me to slow down and see that there are other things going on in her world as well. I developed understanding and I was able to appreciate that other people have got things going on and the world doesn't revolve around me. I stopped being selfish, I was able to see that selfishness where before it was a blind spot to me.

What are you up to in the world now Chris?

I'm letting people know about Beyond Truth, a community business I cofounded. Beyond Truth is an organization that me and my friends started from with the understanding of Beyond Recovery. We want to bring the understanding to the community to help crime prevention. To let others know that there are other options instead of 'the road' (a life of crime). Despite your background and things you've been involved with you can get through the hard times, doing the best you can in the moment. We want to help people see that you can't put everything on your mother or your father or the past, you have to start to take some responsibility for your current behaviours. And we're trying to spread the word that love is everywhere. As I said, you can find it in the darkest places, because love is everywhere.

I'm also trying to broaden my property maintenance business. Hopefully, once I accomplish what I need to do, I can help prisoners that are coming out to reintegrate back into life and work. One of the things I've been trying to live right now is to be the best version of myself I can be every single day.

About Beyond Truth
www.beyondtruth.co.uk
You can find Beyond Truth on Facebook @Beyondtruth5

Jamie Smart

"There are those in this world who believe miracles do not happen. I can assure such skeptics that they do. With hope and faith as beacons, anything can happen."
Syd Banks from The Missing Link

Video transcript

The following is an edited transcription of Jamie answering a question from one of his training delegates exploring the characteristics and nature of stillness, love, resilience, truth, and calm.

Jamie
Here's how it looks to me - you know how if you're watching a movie at the cinema, there is a screen, and the movie is projected on the screen. It doesn't matter what the movie is about, what horrible scenes are played out in the movie or hilarious scenes, tear-jerking scenes, or raunchy scenes. The screen is unaffected. And there's no movie that's so scary or raunchy or troubling that the screen just goes, 'wow I can't handle this, I'm out'. The screen is cool with it all. Well, as I see it, and this is just a metaphor obviously, who we really are is the screen.

And I'll tell you a story. About a year and a half ago, I sit down to read The Missing Link book. When I first read it, I wasn't impacted by it and then I looked at it again, maybe six years later and still no impact. In 2009 I looked at it again and, wow, I saw something in the book. I picked it up again about 15 months ago, to have a read one night, and I thought I'll start at the beginning. I start with the introduction, which is one page with four sentences on it. A couple of sentences are

"There are those in this world who believe miracles do not happen. I can assure such skeptics that they do. With hope and faith as beacons, anything can happen."

Now, I've never been overly keen on the word miracle. I'm not even that keen on the word faith. I've always been much more of the, I'd rather know something. I liked hope because there have been plenty of times when a bit of hope came in handy. As I read these sentences suddenly, I fell out of all this thinking that hadn't even looked like thinking it had just looked like my game plan for life. My accumulated knowledge and understanding so far of the world, and me, work, business, people, relationships and all this stuff I know. It wasn't like I was feeling bad and I read this thing and then I fell out of this thinking. I was just having a 'Jamie' day and things were as they were and I felt fine about it and I had various things I was preoccupied with and various things I was excited about, but I had my game plan for living. So, I read this sentence and suddenly, I fall awake to the moment, I fall out of all that thinking that didn't look like thinking.

What seemed like a long time later but was probably about a second and a half, I'm back in the room with an amazing feeling of peace, well-being, and clarity. What was in my head when I came back was, oh, you're going to have a beautiful life and work you love, and you don't even need to know how it's going to happen. I thought, holy shit, that's not my usual game plan! My usual game plan is, as long as I know exactly how it's going to happen this could just work out okay right? like, no, you're going to have a beautiful life, work you love and you don't even need to know how it's going to happen.

Here's the funny thing, I was listening to an interview with a psychedelic scientist, doing psychedelic experiments around things like curing PTSD and addictions with psychedelics. This is research in the US that was banned for decades and so they're doing it again research with LSD and psilocybin. I was listening to it and he said something really interesting; He said that in the cases where it worked, each time the people had a healing experience as a result from taking a psychedelic it was as a result of having a mystical experience; a spiritual experience. They've got this thing, which is an empirical scale, which is called the mystical experience scale. It's a scientific scale used for evaluating spiritual experiences or what they call mystical experiences and they have six qualities.

The first is kind of the dissolution of time and space like being thrown fully into the now. The second is a sense of connection to everything and everyone. The third is what William James described as the noetic experience. The noetic experience is the sense that what you're experiencing is more true than everyday life. That's what I would call a spiritual fact. When you fall out of your maps, models, and ideas about yourself and about life in the world and fall awake to the truth of the moment. That experience and insight often or typically has that noetic quality; that sense of being even more true than what you know in everyday life; despite the fact that you couldn't prove it by showing your work and doing the math and that sort of thing.

So, I come back to the present. I have that sense that what I just realized is truer than all my ideas about the world which looked pretty true and real and reliable, and it stayed with me. I spend a decent amount of each day caught up in the world of how I think it works and all my usual insecurities and preoccupations. When I think about what I realized, you're going to have a beautiful life and work you love, you don't even need to know how it's going to happen. I see that's true. Can I prove it? no, but I know, I know.

So, I think what happens is for a heartbeat you fall out of the movie and catch a glimpse of the screen. Then when you come back to so called reality a heartbeat later, or an infinity later, when someone says, what was it like, what you're left with is love, peace stillness. When you were there it was just 'ahhhhhhh', but we describe the after effect using those terms.

Those terms like resilience, what does that mean? It's the ability to bounce back. As we're talking about bouncing back that's happening in time and space, but who you really are is before time and space. It looks to me that those qualities that we often attribute to True Self to who we really are. If we're being precise about it, there the world of form after effects or side effects or manifestations of the knowledge of who we really are.

That's how it's looking to me today. Bear in mind all these things I'm saying they're just kind of metaphors trying to get a handle on something that is before time, space matter and handles.

About Jamie Smart
Jamie Smart is a Sunday Times bestselling author, speaker and coach. He's passionate about sharing the principles behind clarity and awakening people to their innate capacity for clarity, resilience and wellbeing. He's the author of 5 books, including the bestsellers CLARITY, RESULTS and The Little Book of Clarity. You can reach him at www.JamieSmart.com or in the usual social media places on the handle @jamiesmartcom

Colin Pitcairn

"Love is everywhere."
Colin Pitcairn

I met Colin a few years ago when I was working for a charity supporting informal carers. Colin had been struggling with fear and anxiety for over 30 years, but he was open to change. In order to explain about true nature and unconditional love I told him the story of the parrot & owl. I'd been given this metaphor to use in my work by my psychotherapy supervisor, Elizabeth Barr. I use the metaphor often as it is so relatable for many people including myself. The story isn't written down but rather passed from person to person in a bespoke way to suit the needs of that person. Below I attempt to put the metaphor into written form, with Elizabeth's consent.

The metaphor of the parrot & the owl

We each have two inner birds guiding our lives but in very different ways. One is a noisy and insistent parrot, and the other is an owl which is quieter, but a wise and gentle guide.

The parrot seems to live in our heads bossing us around with its great ideas and drama stories. The parrot likes to point out all the things that have and could go wrong. Sometimes it likes to tell us how great we are and other times it shows us every area where we just don't match up to its high and unrealistic expectations. The parrot is fear based and although it thinks it is being a friend and keeping us safe, it is really misguided and is only interested in protecting itself. One minute my parrot is telling me how great I am and the next minute it is pointing out what a loser I am – which is true? The answer is neither, both are musings of an insecure parrot trying to feel secure and regain power.

Clients often ask how they can get rid of the parrot. The parrot loves drama so any attention we give it, good or bad, feeds it and gives it strength. Rather than getting rid of it the goal is to see the parrot for what it is – part of the human function repeating old, stale unhelpful patterns given to it through conditioning. The parrot has a loud voice, but it has no ability to make us do anything it is shouting about. The parrot hates the now – it finds its strength in time travelling to the past and the future. This is because in the now we have the greatest access to the wisdom of the owl and the parrot loses its ability to seemingly have power over us. The more we begin to notice the parrot at play we can wake up to the moment, fall out of its trance and regain our power in the now.

The Owl lives deep inside of us and it is made of wisdom and unconditional love. The owl will tell us things that will truly look after us, it has our best interests at heart all the time. The owl will tell us what is needed in any situation, like a wise and intelligent inner satellite navigation system. The owl will never let us down and is always trying to guide us by wisdom even when we don't notice it. The owl is reliable and can be trusted even if we have ignored it for years – it doesn't hold grudges like the parrot. The owl lives firmly in the now and is grounded in the truth of reality not the imaginations of past and future.

You might experience the owl as a big insight that changes your life, a moment of clarity, a good feeling state, a moment of peace, a great idea from nowhere, an inner knowing, or you simply find your body doing the next best thing to do in that particular moment. The owl's wisdom is specific to you in that exact situation so it can't be given to you by someone else ahead of time. Others can point you to the owl, wake you up to learn to tune in and to trust that wise guidance is always there.

The owl can be accessed in any moment but to begin with it certainly seems to be easier to 'hear' its guidance when we are in a calm state with a clearer mind. So, begin to get to know the characteristics and habits of your inner birds to help guide you from a life of fear and confusion to one of peace and inner contentment.

Colin's Story in his own words.

Before I found wise owl, my GPS was off centre, and the parrot seemed to have a lot of power over me, messing with my head.

For thirty years I thought I was broken.

Then Nicola Drew came into my life and she has helped me change my life and to find the real me.

Now I know I'm not broken, what a relief!

The parrot was telling me lies and I learned that it is not to be trusted. Before I knew this, I thought that I had to believe everything that the parrot was telling me. I was scared and exhausted by it. Now I know that the wise owl is always there to guide me and will never let me down I can live more of the time from peace. The parrot hasn't disappeared and still looks for gaps when my state of mind is not so clear to tell me fear based stories, but I notice what is going on and I listen for the wise owl.

I notice that the parrot's stories look much more real and true when I am feeling stressed or overwhelmed. Nicola also taught me the 7/11 breathing technique which helps to calm me down so I can see through the parrot's drama. Having this breathing technique which works so quickly and so well has stopped me being so frightened. I can trust the intelligent system in the moment and don't need to overthink what might happen in the future as I have access to inner wisdom and more control over the stress response.

I love life!

Big Col

7/11 Breathing Technique
Colin mentions 7/11 breathing. This is a powerful breathing technique in which the out breath is longer than the in breath. For example, breath in for the count of 7 and out for the count of 11. This longer out breath activates the relaxation response at times when we may be about to go into or be in the stress response. It is very simple but very effective.

You can find more details here.
www.hgi.org.uk/resources/delve-our-extensive-library/resources-and-techniques/7-11-breathing-how-does-deep

George Halfin

"Love and understanding harmonize the mind of humanity to its true nature"
Syd Banks

To me love is the ability to go beyond the noisy commentary of our thinking (about who we are with, what's happening now, our feelings etc) and be fully present and in the moment with that person or group of people from an open place of curiosity and connection.

It's the 'ultimate connection'. You communicate essence to essence with your whole being with and without words. When you communicate in this way there are no barriers because when we see ourselves as part of humanity and not as individuals, we are all connected. It is only our thinking in that moment that divides us. There is a simplicity and beauty, curiosity and connectedness in communication and a feeling of love is ever present.

I have seen this in the work I have done co-facilitating a peer support group for gay and bi men struggling with issues of sex, drugs and alcohol. Where in spite of their initial thoughts about why a woman was co-facilitating the group they saw - through me showing up open minded, without judgement and talking honestly from my own different but relatable experiences- that we all have habits of thinking that express themselves in our own 'special' ways.

I have seen this in the Nisa Nashim Jewish Muslim women's group I co-chair and the subsequent wellbeing sessions I have co-facilitated with the wider network of women at different life stages to my own.

I experienced it on the 24/7 In Search of A Peaceful Mind Zoom room which I volunteered for one hour a week when anyone in the world could just show up looking for support and benefit from the love and wisdom that flows from speaking essence to essence.

I'm not saying that we should be under the illusion that people don't have very different experiences of the world both lived and historic, that derives from our nationality, age, gender, sexuality, race, religion, political views etc that make up our own unique identities. I'm saying that when you come from a place of love, respect, openness, curiosity and shared humanity it provides a space for honest discourse where emotions can be shared without judgement in a way that may not otherwise have been possible. When people communicate from this place conversations that can change the way we see the world and others in it can happen. They can also help educate and change the views of those who see these conversations.

I experienced this recently after watching 'Question It' on YouTube where a group of friends from the creative industries got together to talk openly about the realities of being black and mixed race in the UK today. Watching this conversation that was imbued with the sense of mutual respect and connection, with a complete lack of judgement about any comments made by anyone taking part, made me laugh, cringe and confront my own unseen ignorance and behaviours and also start to see what I could do differently and how I could educate my children in the future.

In a world which can seem increasingly divided these essence to essence conversations where people speak from their own true nature with unconditional love have the power to bring people together in shared humanity. To know this and to explore this more deeply and know others are doing the same, gives me hope for challenges we as a planet face today.

Much love

About George Halfin
George Halfin is an Innate Health coach and Innovation Projects lead currently working for Terrence Higgins Trust (Europe's largest HIV and Sexual Health charity). She is Co-chair of Nisa Nashim Essence (part of Nisa Nashim a national network, which brings Jewish and Muslim women together across the UK to inspire and lead social change.). An Associate of Unstoppable! a Three Principles career and coaching business. She is passionate about supporting people to see beyond their preconceived limitations for themselves and the good of society. Contact: halfingeorge@googlemail.com

Mary-Beth Tighe

"We are not human beings having a spiritual experience-we are spiritual beings having a human experience."
Pierre Teilhard de Chardin

Goodbye Grrr

When I was asked to contribute to this book, I was initially overwhelmed with so many emotions, good and bad. For a brief moment I questioned why anything I might say would be worth telling. That thought passed and I was back to feeling overwhelmed with pure love. The life experiences we are going through can be challenging, yet if we are willing to be curious about the path we are on it can lead to a joyous adventure.

Making my way toward a free mind has been gradual. For years I had the negative feeling of Grrr in my soul due to childhood and early adulthood events. It would manifest itself as anger and intolerance, including a high expectation of myself and others. I pride myself on being self-aware and quite intuitive, yet I could not stop the Grrr when it made an appearance.

My interest in wanting to know more began after a once in a lifetime experience: a four day trek to the ancient Machu Picchu citadel in Peru. This was an extremely difficult challenge for me (both physically and mentally), and I confronted a lot of my fears. Totally unexpectedly-- but with extreme clarity--I realised that upon returning from Peru my Grrr had departed.   This was my first insight.

Luckily for me my uplifting friend Nicola and I had discussions about my spiritual adventure, and she introduced me to the Three Principles wisdom. Nicola reminded me that our true self never leaves us and is more powerful than the Grrr will ever be. I continued on this path by reading and listening for inspiration while also being receptive to reinvesting in my deeper truths to increase my well being.

All I can say is: Wow! My awareness of Mind, Consciousness and Thought has led me back to my true nature. I have let go of the past and live very much in the now. I no longer have any expectations of myself and others. I am more positive and resilient. I love myself more every day. I know the Three Principles can and do enhance a person's life experiences and enrich relationships. My Grrr has been replaced with peace.

My husband, son and friends have noticed I am much better at dealing with all life's experiences, both good and bad. It is because of my willingness to be curious and an affirmation that unconditional love has always been a part of me. I must also thank my Grandma B, Maw Maw, Mother and Aunt M for providing a lasting imprint of the true nature and unconditional love which I have returned to and intend to live by forever. My insights continue to be rewarding and provide me with a deeper sense of purpose.

My future goals include continuing my human experience full of love for myself and others. I am eager to play my part in leading by example living the Three Principles and looking forward to many more transformative moments. Without realising the deep and heartfelt impact of her valuable words to me, Nicola Drew once said: "The biggest gift we can give the world is to deepen our understanding, live in alignment with the understanding and model how life really works."

Live Laugh Love
MB

Palma Michel

*"There is nothing more important to true growth than
realising that you are not the voice of the mind - you are the
one who hears it."*
Michael A. Singer

The one thing that I would like everyone to know about their
true nature is that your true nature is inherently whole, at
peace and unconditionally loving. Reconnecting with your true
nature, the silent space within that is always and already here
as the gap between your thoughts is the best thing you can
ever do for yourself. Inner peace or wholeness is not
something special that you need to attain and you also don't
need to heal yourself first as you already have inner peace
and you are already whole, no matter how broken you might
think you are. Inner peace only feels elusive as most of us are
looking to find it in all the wrong places. We look to the external
world and we look to the noisy parts of our experience, our
thoughts and feelings. Then we try to change our thoughts
and feelings in an attempt to feel better, yet by doing that we
often make ourselves feel worse. All these experiences would
not be possible without your awareness, a silent witnessing
quality, that it is always there in the background. My invitation
to you is to allow all your experiences to be as they are and
instead start to notice the small gaps between your thoughts
like the gaps between the words that you are reading right
now. Start noticing the silence in between sounds and the
small gap between your inhale and your exhale. It is within
these gaps that your true nature reveals itself.

This deeper understanding has changed everything in my life
and benefitted all areas in my life. It was like coming home,
noticing that the safest, most peaceful, joyful, most loving

place was inside of me and is always there, irrespective of my thoughts, feelings and of what is going on in the world. Operating from this place of presence, everything feels quite effortless. I have become more creative, my relationships have become deeper, I look younger, my health is much better and people even feel that I have a calming effect on them.

About Palma Michel
I work at the intersection of high performance and peak wellbeing as a transformative coach and mindfulness teacher. My clients include organisations like CNN, PWC, The LSE, CEOs, entrepreneurs, creatives and everyday people who are working through burnout or a life threatening illness. I also host The Explorer's Mind Podcast, which inspires and empowers you to live a meaningful and deeply fulfilled life.

More information at www.palmamichel.com
Connect with me via email palma@palmamichel.com IG @palmamichel_ twitter @herenowalltime

Marnix Pauwels

"We are most alive when we're in love."
John Updike

Interview

What would you love the world to know about true nature and unconditional love?

I'd like people to know that they don't have to look for true nature and unconditional love outside of who they already are. That it's the most reliable guide in their life. Neglecting that will mean they will get all these nudges and hints in order to wake up and look in the right direction. Knowing about true nature gives you an additional option in life, because it changes the whole dynamics of reactivity that most people have. Whenever something occurs to you, a feeling, an emotion, a thought, an idea about an activity, most people don't realize that they have the opportunity to just stay with that for a while. To give themselves space to go in the other direction if that feels better. We don't have to act on everything that happens to us, that we feel, that occurs to us. We can always stay with the thing that never changes within us and listen for the best answer, the best solution, the best idea.

The more you get a feel for the thing within you that never changes the easier life gets, because everything changes when it comes to events, bodies, stories, futures, relationships, jobs, bank accounts. There's one thing that never changes and the more you get to see that and experience that for yourself, the more you feel grounded in life And the more you feel in touch with all the beautiful stuff that we were born with, things like playfulness, creativity, wonder, curiosity and resilience. We have that and being true to who we really are, opens that up again. It's not gone, you don't have to look for it. You don't have to travel to find it, you can find it wherever you are.

The only thing is, it's so obvious and it's so close, it's the first thing we overlook. It's the most subtle thing in the world. We're used to looking for things that aren't subtle. We look for changing things, for loud things, for obvious things. The true nature of who you are is constantly there. That's why we don't see it. What is always there, you just don't notice, you don't recognize it, but you can.

When true nature, the thing that never changes within you recognizes itself, it's like a whole new world of possibilities opens up where you can enjoy a natural confidence that's not built on behavior or the way you dress or the way you look. It's simply built on an intrinsic trust you have, and you'll find your creativity and you'll be less inclined to bury it. You'll feel like you must share it. You're not afraid to share it because you know that you inherently, who you really are, will never be broken or hurt or scratched by anything that anybody will ever tell you.

It's a gift we've been carrying around all our lives and that we just overlook. It's a gift that keeps on giving, the more you respect it, the more you feel from where you rely on it, the more you connect to it. It always gets deeper and deeper and makes you more relaxed and more in love with life. Knowing who we truly are, makes us really fall in love with life again.

How has seeing this more deeply changed your world?

This has opened up my world. I lived in a very dark place for a very long time. That was my status quo, my normal and I didn't know that it was even possible to enjoy life. I really didn't because I was so afraid of how temporary everything was that I didn't allow myself to feel good, even for a minute. I micromanaged my misery. Whenever I felt good, I changed the feeling by starting to think miserable things because I didn't think I deserved the good feeling.

But what understanding gave me is an endless appreciation for life instead of a large, smelly pile of distrust, cynicism, arrogance, fear, depression and all these frantic behaviors to deal with it in the short term. I was addicted to alcohol for 28 years, simply because I didn't know how to deal with my uncomfortable feelings. I learned to stay connected to who I truly am which means that I got to feel a direct experience with the fleeting nature of everything that happens to me. In turn, I stopped being afraid of those feelings.

Before I was always afraid about what would be waiting for me around the corner. Now I'm running to the corner like yeah, bring it. It has made my life lighter, simpler, more direct, more in the now, more creative, more fluid. I'm more caring, or at least I am not scared to show that I care. I probably was already caring but I didn't see that as a good thing. I care more and I am more interested in people. I didn't like people at all, I didn't trust them. I started to like people, to appreciate people and get curious. I got curious about life in general, about my opportunities and my potential.

After a 30-year career in advertising, I went into coaching. I completely flipped my life. I quit drinking, quit smoking, quit using drugs. My anxiety disappeared, for 15 years, I was very anxious and had a lot of panic attacks. My depression completely vanished; I had been depressed for 20 years almost non-stop. My addictions went away. It took some time to get comfortable with being uncomfortable but that's something I had to learn. I didn't learn that earlier as I started drinking when I was 14. I had no developed grownups skills when it came to dealing with life.

I came from a very dark place and the light has been flipped on. Then I saw that I was in a place with a lot of mess. I had to rearrange and get rid of all kinds of stuff because that's one thing I think I really underestimated when I quit drinking, I thought I would be fine from there. A deeper understanding gave me the courage to deal with whatever it was I had to deal with and to really appreciate the simple fact of being alive.

It gave me all the courage in the world, seeing who I truly am, it gave me all the courage in the world to discover my possibilities, my potential. I saw the power we all have inside of us. It made me a more likeable person, a more interested person, and more patient than I was. I enjoy life, daily, without connecting it to any activity. It's like, life feels amazing just the way it is. Then there are lots of cool things happening as well, that's the bonus. I discovered the aliveness of being a human being without the intense fear of all the things that don't exist. The aliveness feeds me, nourishes me, and gives me all this inspiration to live an open and grateful life.

About Marnix Pauwels

I coach and I've been coaching for maybe six, seven years, but professionally about three years. I've written books on mental health, depression, anxiety and addiction. It's very helpful that I have suffered from all this myself. Mostly because people trust me quicker, my story is helpful. For me it feels like I've been bound and gagged for 42 years and it was suddenly released. It's out of gratefulness; that's one of the reasons I do what I do. It feels like I have been given a second chance to live a completely different life in every respect, like literally in every respect.

I see this in my clients, people become more radiant, more alive and the dullness goes away, and they begin to shine. That's what happens when people, in any way, begin to shed the idea that they are what they think they are. There's this aliveness that has enough room to play again. That's so amazing! I think many people are looking for reliability, for safety for something to stand on but they look for it in things that constantly change. People say they want peace of mind or they want to know how to make decisions or they want a better job, but all they hope is deep inside to have this feeling of universal connection again.

www.marnix.nl

Gary Bridgeman

"Wisdom is knowing I am nothing,
Love is knowing I am everything,
and between the two my life moves."
Nisargadatta Maharaj

What is unconditional love?

The answer depends on who is asking.

For the separate self, unconditional love is something that it searches for and wants in relationships.

A love without conditions, total acceptance by the other.

The separate self goes out and looks for love in the world of things, trying to find this love in one thing or another.

But the thing about unconditional love is that is a contradiction wanting love without conditions is, in fact, a condition.

Something we impose on the other.

And because of this, unconditional love doesn't exist for the separate self.

It will never find love without conditions because it will always come with conditions.

The separate self says I don't know what unconditional love is, but I know what it isn't - and so will keep searching for something that can't be found.

But in the absence of a person, there is only love without conditions.

If you want to call that unconditional love go ahead, here, I say that love beyond conditions is just love.

Pure consciousness is nothing but love.

When you know the true self then love with or without conditions is irrelevant, you are beyond labels, categories or nouns.

You are pure awareness, pure acceptance, and you see the inherent perfection in all things.

And that is what we are searching for not the emotion, not the momentary feeling in our body but the deeper knowing of who we truly are.

And within that space of knowing relationships happen and they come with their conditions, their expectations, their baggage, their dreams and their fears.

But now they are held by something more profound, a peace that stretches on and on, a warm embrace of everything that is.

You no longer need the other to complete you, to provide you with a love that fulfils you.

Because the other is you, there is no separation here.

Everything is allowed, love without conditions does not judge anything, and it is impossible for the intellect to work this out and imagine such a space exists.

It makes up a story about what unconditional love looks like, who it needs to be to get it, and why it will never be good enough to deserve unconditional love.

It makes up expectations and believes that unconditional love is out of reach.

It believes that this space of oneness is filled with rainbows, unicorns, dancing lights and rapturous feelings.

And isn't the simplicity of pure awareness.

Others have said that awakening is the realisation of the absence of a separate self, of the emptiness and the void.

And liberation is the realisation that the emptiness is full of love that has no conditions.

Sometimes these things come at once; sometimes, liberation takes some time to arrive.

But when it comes there are no words to describe the experience fully since as soon as you try to talk about it; you are no longer in it.

Nothing changes but everything is different.

Pure awareness is the acceptance of all things as they are before the intellect gets involved and starts adding conditions or caveats onto love.

But once liberation is realised, you bring love to all your situations and your happiness can't be determined by or be dependent on an object.

You can hold the tragedy and beauty of the world in perfect balance in this space of equanimity.

And now you play your part, enter the flow of life and life unfolds without the need to control or change any of it.

And you already know this experience of love.

When the separate self collapses and you fall into the space of being.

No matter what the object of our love we all have had a moment in our lives where we have felt this pure love, this sense of being without separation.

We believe that this experience is coming from the object but it is coming from within you, generated by you.

You don't need to go and find this love out there in the world of things.

It is right here.

You have always been everything that you are looking for.

About Gary Bridgeman
Gary is a life guide, meditation and yoga teacher, but mostly is a human being trying to make sense of life just like you.

He is not a trained philosopher, nor has he followed any particular school of wisdom, although he has picked up qualifications in psychology, coaching, counselling, yoga, and meditation along the way.

He is just someone who has had a full range of experiences in life.

From early age trauma, depression, suicidal thoughts, psychedelics, addiction, anxiety, parenthood, failed relationships, and even bankruptcy as well as hours spent on books, coaching, counselling, and courses that have added to his knowledge.

He shares from this experience on the nature of consciousness and being human.

Connect with him at www.garybridgeman.me

David Hill

"Between stimulus and response there is a space. In that space lies our power to choose our response. In our own response lies our growth and our freedom."
Viktor Frankl

What would you love the world to know about true nature and unconditional love?

What a great question. One of the biggest things that I have seen when it comes to love is that I had innocently bundled love up into different categories: love for my family, romantic love, love of my friends, love of my rugby team, love for my dog... the categories were almost endless. What an understanding of the Three Principles has allowed me to see at a deeper level, is that love is just connection between two or more beings, and that the feeling that comes with it is only felt through a reflection of our own thoughts.

What do I mean by that? At times in the past I thought I needed to be loved by someone else in order to feel love. If you think about that as a statement, it can't possibly be true as it requires love to be given by someone for someone else to feel it; where would it start? This seemingly tiny misunderstanding by me would tie me in knots at times. When I saw with absolute clarity, that love is unconditional – no ifs, no buts – then there was no longer any need for the categorisation process that I applied to love. This led to feeling a deeper, more open and infinite pool of love at my disposal that, I could show more often, to anyone, in the knowledge that it wasn't a resource that I could run out of.

If more people knew this simple fact then the world would be a more compassionate, loving and forgiving place; now that has to be something worth sharing!

How has this deeper seeing changed your world?

Seeing the absolute truth in this has allowed me to try things that I might have been scared of doing in the past, in the knowledge that I can't hurt anyone when my intentions come from unconditional love.

Yes, it's made family life feel less stressful and is allowing me to be a more compassionate parent as my children reach their teens, but the main change is I'm only ever me, living a life without needing to put on a different persona for different situations. Being authentic and honest in everything I do has had a positive effect on what I'm doing in the world, but in a very subtle way.

I work in two very different worlds: financial services project management and as a coach, focusing mainly on veteran's mental health. This understanding has allowed me to trust my instincts more and most importantly surface them with others. In the past I would feel what was right and then get ambushed by my personal thinking which would start beating the idea down and, in the end, I would step back from sharing it with the world. Now I trust myself much more and if it feels like the right thing to do or say, then I'll bring it up.

The flip of that is also true. I no longer feel the anxious requirement to make sure my voice is heard in meetings. If I don't have anything valuable to add, the best I can do for everyone is to continue to listen until I see something of value to contribute. How many meetings have we been in when there's a bun fight to get ideas heard and end up achieving very little...

In my work with veterans I know that despite what they are currently feeling emotionally via the thoughts that are playing in their minds, that they are 100% mentally healthy underneath that noise. This means we don't need to dig into the content of their thoughts and can concentrate on the far less personal idea around how our human experience is created. This is driving conversations based on hope, rather than on strategies to cope with and manage symptoms, a fundamental shift in direction.

Understanding unconditional love is a very powerful thing and touches every part of our lives. The simplicity and the hope that it brings to our lives and the lives of those around us is profound.

About David Hill
I was a soldier for 17 years in the British Army and since leaving in 2013 I have worked for Amazon and currently work for Standard Life Aberdeen.

Part of my military role encompassed the absolute privilege of being trusted with the lives and welfare of a number of others. In my Regiment, The RIFLES, we have an unwritten motto of "Once a Rifleman, always a Rifleman" and it's something I firmly believe in. When my phone started ringing with requests for help with my friends' mental health, I knew I had to do something and trusted my instincts to know what was right.

Four years ago, I had my own mental health struggles but, I knew in the darkest moment that it was just that, a moment, and that it would pass. I also decided to listen to the advice I'd been giving others; giving myself space and time to take stock, and importantly to be open with a few friends. On my journey to rediscovering my mental health I was introduced to the Three Principles and I knew instantly I had found an idea that could reduce the pain and suffering felt by my friends.

Since then I have trained as a practitioner with One Thought, reduced the days I work for Standard Life Aberdeen, partnered with a small military charity, Just RIFLES, and now formerly support veterans in my spare time. Most of this work is 1-1, but I have just started a small group via Zoom. The idea being to share this understanding to empower others to feel confident and able to share with their friends and hopefully create a community that look out for each other.

I have also set up a small coaching practice called Simplicity in Mind, where I offer coaching to corporate and private clients in order to fill the gap in my income as a result of working reduced hours. I have delivered a number of 1-1 sessions in person and across the globe via Zoom, as well as talking to larger groups at Standard Life Aberdeen and for the Scottish Government.

If you're interested in what I'm doing and want to learn more please drop me an email: dave@simplicityinmind.co.uk

www.justrifles.co.uk/about/get-help-now
www.simplicityinmind.co.uk

Lorraine Turnpenny

*"Your thoughts are like the artist's brush. They create a
personal picture of the reality you live in."*
Sydney Banks

Love is the answer

Don't be fooled by the many masks I wear, none of them are
the real me. Don't be fooled by my bubbly personality, I avoid
people and parties when I struggle to put on a happy face.
Don't be fooled by the confident and cool exterior, behind this
lurks depression and loneliness.

I covered up a deep sadness that I'd missed out on being a
mother. That had turned to more regret that I would never be
a grandmother as I got older. There was nothing anyone could
say to make me feel better about this; I'd messed up, marriage
and miscarriages, and the pain was stuck in my throat
protecting my heart. I lived alone with these thoughts. I think
my friend Ange is suspicious and includes me in sweet
activities with her gorgeous granddaughter. I have the best
friends in the world.

Bloomin' 'eck I didn't see this coming! Wow!

I was at work when I received a baby scan in a text message.
My older brother Lee and his beautiful Spanish girlfriend,
Laura, were expecting a baby and the whole family were in
shock.

When I got home from work I crawled under the duvet and
sobbed until I fell asleep. I felt the grief and self-pity I'd held

so tightly gradually drain away. The next day I awoke full of unconditional love for my family, and for myself.

I'd adored being Auntie Lorraine to four boisterous boys by marriage and they were all grown men now. In this off-the-scale exciting turn of events Auntie Lorraine gets to ride again! In Spain! I'd better start learning Spanish!

I was thrilled about the baby, a baby boy, and couldn't wait to meet Laura and bump. I never want to forget the day my stepdad, Roy, and I picked them up from the airport and the evening that followed. So much excitement and laughter filled the air as Mum, Roy, and I showered them with love and baby gifts. I was in complete awe and amazement at this new life in our family. I can only describe the feeling in the room as magical. It felt other-worldly, intoxicating, like riding a giant wave of love and happiness. I think my brother felt it too, he was holding back tears.

I choke with emotion as I write this. You see, I hadn't felt this state of unpolluted and unconditional love for my family for a long time. I dreamed of the perfect happy family but when we got together there was often tension. And yet there I was enjoying the moment with them, not reacting from our checkered past nor anticipating problems. I realized there and then that life didn't need to be so hard; I had touched pure consciousness where anything is possible and anxious thinking doesn't cloud the view. I knew everything would be okay, and that it always was.

A few months later my heart cracked open with the news of the birth of my nephew Luca. I cried again, this time tears of relief, compassion and joy for our family.

Dreams really do come true.

Lorraine (Tía Favorita)

About Lorraine Turnpenny
Lorraine is a Wellbeing Practitioner in Leicestershire, UK.

Susan Marmot

*"Everyone in the world shares
the same innate source of wisdom, but it is hidden by the
tangle of our own misguided personal thoughts."*
Syd Banks, The Missing Link

What would you love the world to know about true nature and unconditional love?

That they are innate in us already we don't have to go and find them or eternally work on ourselves to try and make ourselves better humans. We are already everything we have ever been looking for, we just lose sight of that and go off searching in unhelpful directions that take us further away from our true nature not closer to it.

I innocently did that for years, trying harder and harder to feel okay to be okay to fix myself. I thought if I just go on one more course/training/therapy maybe then I will be healed but the search never ended, and I felt I could not be fixed.

When I look back now there was nothing much wrong with me I just thought there were a lot of things wrong with me which led me to feel that way a lot of the time. Ultimately there was nothing fundamentally wrong with me. What I had was a thinking problem and once I figured that out, I was free and my true nature was able to shine though without me getting in the way all the time.

My mind got quieter naturally and in that peace a ton of helpful gifts showed up, one of them being the ability to feel more. More love for me, more love for everyone. I understood people better once I understood more about how all minds work.

In the peace I dropped into a loving, unconditional space that I find myself dropping in to whenever I am working, it is a oneness where my judgements drop away and I feel a profound and loving connection.

How has this deeper seeing changed your world?

It has enabled me to see and feel deeply where detachment existed before.

It has given me a flow in my life where stuckness existed before.

It has given me a knowing where confusion and indecisiveness existed before.

It has given me connection where separation and aloneness existed before.

It has given me contentedness where dissatisfaction existed before.

It has given me the ability to listen fresh where staleness and 'thinking I knew' existed before.

It has given me everything I was searching for when lacking existed before.

It has given me an easy, connected, loving relationship where hurt existed before.

It has enabled me to live happily where depression and anxiety existed before.

It has enabled me to live from my heart with purpose and stop fixing myself when brokenness existed before.

About Susan Marmot

Susan is a senior three principles facilitator. She works with people from all different sectors including the criminal justice system and those affected by homelessness, and she also works with private clients. She has helped many people find mental health who have been struggling.

Susan is also is on the faculty of the One Though foundations programme training practitioners.

She co facilitates a Relationship Ready program helping people to find loving relationships.

She loves what she does and is grateful for the freedom of mind she has discovered for herself and is passionate about sharing what she has found so helpful with others.

Dean Rees-Evans

The Universe is Unconditional Love, Love is the Gift
'Wherever you stand, be the Soul of that place.'
Rumi

My story begins early one Sunday morning sitting on a train amid the hustle and bustle of the London underground. I was on my way to another weekend training session with the wonderful Dr. Roger Mills from the Center for Sustainable Change, California. By now we had become very firm and fun friends, and I was feeling not only excitement at what the day had in store for me, but also on seeing dear Roger again, it was always a blessing to be with him, so much fun and laugher and so, so much love.

There were a few of us on the train that morning, my brother Blair, his then girlfriend Jo, and a couple of others. We pulled into yet another station and I was enjoying seeing the people come and go, and feeling so very alive, and in love with life and the world. As the doors opened an elderly Sikh couple boarded the train, she was wearing a beautiful Sari and I distinctly remember the man had a sky blue turban on, and I thought how beautiful they both looked. I said a cheery good morning to them as they sat down opposite me; the woman replied with a nod of the head and eyes demurely downcast, the man beamed a delightful smile and returned the greeting.

And then it happened, the man and I just looked at each other, and we just kept looking, and looking, and it was as life itself was saying: "I see you".

Time passed, I really don't remember how long, and I was

filled with the deepest sense of love and wonder at the beauty of this moment; this undeniable connection, this life confirming sense of 'I honour your humanity, I celebrate your soul, because you and I our one'. And in that feeling of Oneness we both swam in the ocean of unconditional love. There was a magical moment in all this looking where this lovely man raised his hands together palm to palm, as if in prayer, or salutation to the moment, and in such a wonderful and typically Indian manner, his head wobbled from side to side, and with tears in my eyes, I too raised my hands in this mutual salutation.

While we looked on at each other, I suddenly felt someone nudging me: "Hey Dean, we need to get off at this stop!" said the voice of my brother. I got up gathered my things, still looking, still deep in this connection, and smiled as I alighted. I stood on the platform as the train departed and again we saluted each other, or was it simply the Universe. Even now as I write these words, tears well in my eyes, for that moment will remain with me forever, as one of my most fond and beautiful memories of Oneness and of universal love.

A short while before the Three Principles exploded in my Consciousness, I was doing it tough in life, I had just broken up with my girlfriend and the worst part was, that I was also breaking up with her beautiful daughter too, and that was probably the most painful experience I had ever gone through. Relationship breakups, sure they were difficult experiences to pass through, but at least I had some experience of how to handle that. But, losing a child, that was unique to me, and we had built up such a bond over a year and half, that I could hardly live with the pain of our separation. To make things worse, I lived near a primary school, and so at end of day, the tears would flow as fast as the children could run and dance and play on their way home past my balcony. Oh boy, what pain! I didn't know things could hurt this bad. At night, I had to constantly chant (I was a practicing Buddhist at the time) just to get my head straight enough to succumb to the desperate desire to sleep and to forget the agony of this severing of our beautiful, mutual and so unconditional connection of deepest love.

And then in an instant it occurred to me, what I needed to do, I need to write about this love. Two poems flowed like an ocean tide into existence – once these words were in the world I knew I needed to take this priceless gift of unconditional love and share it with the whole world, I just didn't know how I was going to do it. Enter Dr. Roger Mills with the baton of Sydney Banks gift to the world in his hand, and then my life was never the same again, and I had my answer, he passed the baton on to me and I was off on the marathon of life and unconditional love.

Here are the poems:

The Little Princess of the Dawn
Dedicated to JEC for all that she taught me of love

Before you fade almost completely from my life
I write these lines in your praise:

Just as the sun doth rise each morn
So would you with a sunshine that is so much you
Sometimes creeping into the room, hoping for an open eye
Or the covers flung back to welcome you in (how I miss that)
Sometimes sensing the world was still at rest,
When all you wanted was to play…reluctantly – but
Sincerely going back to your room to play –
The toys – so many toys – the shrine, in so many different shapes

Reading – hearing your angelic half fairy-like voice whisper
to the dawn
Those strange musings as you emulated what you felt was
adult –
Not knowing that ears could hear you –
Nor caring – for that is a new art not yet learnt

Coming again so often to check if the world was ready yet
To play with your sweet nature – to open its mind
To the ever-new day – what day was it anyway?
"Is it school today?" you ask having innocence
And no concept whatsoever of time and space – Ah…bliss!
You loved each day anew – yesterday! What of it?
Tomorrow – "when's that? – will it be soon – are we there
yet?"

Am I not still with you by this very token?
Does the heart know time and space?
Does a child's mind ever grow old?
Will I ever see your sunshine again?
Or must I now search for it in other faces and other places –
How I long for you

What a curious thing language is – why do I not 'short' for
you?
Why 'long' – why anything – but love you as I do
With all my heart – with the blazing of the sun this very
moment
Low in the sky, like you early rising, heart afresh
Talking of a time when we two were together – innocent
child of my dreams
Who came to me so long ago, talking endlessly of things
now unremembered, and still a babe

Now again you come back to me in my dreams – sometimes
As you are, a young girl of six, and sometimes older, wiser

But still with sweet voice, gentle nature and the fire of the
sun burning in your heart for life –
Always that golden thread of connection between us

You were mine once, whatever that means, and now
I cannot tell – if only I could see you again – here in the
known world –
With your laughter of love and your questions – endless
questions
Like daisy chains so long they could wrap around the world
several times over

"What did you say?" – those sweet words echo and re-echo
throughout my core, throughout my essence,
Throughout this subjective experience I call my life, mingled
with confusion, lacking in substance,
And reaching back, as if I could, through time and space – to
you, and by these very tears
A child again too, like you – hoping, but knowing all along
There is no hope – only you and I, Here and There.

8th April 2004

All is not Lost
Dedicated to JEC, the child of my dreams, for whom I shall
always love

When you came through that door and down the surgery
steps
I had been taken from you at that time.
When you saw it was me; how our hearts leapt for joy
How you clung to me so tightly – as if to say
"Please don't take him away from me again!"
Crimson red in pain, fear, and love, you held me tight
I assured you it was ok, I was coming too
We held hands for the longest time ever

We played together, we laughed,
We chased at dreams already taken from us
We were given no choice
We were made to stay apart
And though I had saved enough love for you to last a lifetime
Put it up under lock and key for safety,
Made my commitment to you –
On oath, to these very gods of this land

My storehouse has been robbed
Desecrated, smashed, abandoned – emptied
But all is not lost, for remaining is one precious seed
Laying on the bare and barren floor
It is the seed of perfection, the seed of love,
The seed that sits outside of time and space
No need for restraints or conditions of any kind

I shall plant this seed in the garden of my heart
That vast continent, that lush open plane, contained within
its centre
The abundance of the universe –
And there it shall grow, and seed itself and grow again, and
again
Until at last – the whole Eden in all its entirety
Will be full to the brim with the mighty oaks and flowers of
this love I bear

Strong, virulent, unstoppable – always giving to all whom
enter –
Never holding back, never blocking
Ever the seed of perfection being planted in them in return
Until this paradise be the garden that grows in every living
heart the universe has to offer
This is my commitment this is my decree

8th April 2004

About Dean Rees-Evans
Dean studied with Dr Roger Mills from the Center of Sustainable
Change, California in 2004, and with Mr. Sydney Banks.
Beginning his work with Roger in London and later setting up
a partnership with Sue Panciewicz, in his hometown of
Colchester UK. Dean now works in Australia, which he has
made his home.

Dean is as happy hanging out with the kids at school, as he
is in a boardroom with a group of CEO's, or amid nursing
staff at busy hospital. Much of his work these days is via
Zoom due to the current world situation but this doesn't stop
him creating the most ideal conditions for an effective
meeting of minds; helping individuals, couples or small
groups, look in the right direction towards the priceless gift of
psychological freedom.

Dean's first Three Principles based book is written for
teenagers and will be available through Amazon worldwide
in 2020. He is currently working on a second book, which is
a love story.

DeanReesEvans@gmail.com
www.ThreePrinciples.com.au

Helen Amery

"We are love, and there's nothing we can do to change that. Love Is our very nature. It's what we are when we no longer believe our own stories."
Byron Katie

I've spent a lot of my career working with leaders and teams. When you ask a team 'what would make this team great' you get the same kind of answers everywhere you go – to be listened to, to listen, to care about each other, to have fun, to be creative, to not judge or be judged, to collaborate, to be proactive not reactive.

And of course the reason the answers are so consistent is because this is who we know ourselves to be. These are how true nature expresses itself. And all naturally available the more we recognise this and see that this is what we are by default.

That's it really. Anything and everything else we've said and done has layered more story over the top of this. But why have we done that?

I guess it's because we don't like the feeling of being out of alignment with our nature. Out of alignment is frustration and stress and anxiety and incapability and not-enough-ness. But really, the yukkiness of that misaligned feeling is perfect because it's designed to alert us to the fact we've become misaligned. If it was a lovely feeling we wouldn't pay attention to it.

The problem has come about because we've got confused believing that the yukkiness is telling us there's something genuinely wrong and that we need to fix it. We've been a bit like a novice plumber with a hammer and a wrench and we've gone about trying to bash things back into shape to get the system working again.

In doing this – little did we know – we were actually maintaining a poor-flowing water supply. We weren't improving things, and sometimes our bashing and twisting of the pipes caused the water to flow even slower than it did before we started.

Which is fine. We don't need to worry about this. Just like a pipe that has a kink and has pressurised water coming through, the water will find a way out somewhere or other. Whether it's a weakness in the metal or at a join between pipes, something will give and true nature will burst back through, restoring the system to flow.

What becomes available, the more we see the design of our emotional plumbing system, is to know to keep our hands off the pipework! We start to recognise that, compared to the intelligence of life, we really don't know what we're doing. We see over and over again how the water flow restores perfectly well the less we're involved. And we start to see that the discomfort of the experience is unconditional love telling us we're lost and out of alignment. We've temporarily lost sight of our default setting by believing a temporary thought to be a gospel truth.

And now there's nothing to do except see this and know that true nature has got it. Including if it looks like we're taking ourselves further into twisted pipes, it's still OK, it's still got us.

Having seen this for myself, the biggest impact in my life has been my experience with my kids. It really looked before like they were rude or disrespectful if they weren't listening to me.

It really looked like there was a problem if they were stressed or upset. It really looked like my safety required them to be a certain way.

Instead, the more I've seen what's really going on, the more I've seen that they are also fine in their experience, no matter what it is. I've seen when they're lost with their hammers and wrenches and that it's not going to be a great time to engage with them. I've also seen how the pipework sorts itself out and they bob back up to the surface. Every. Single. Time.

It doesn't mean it's pretty. It doesn't mean it's without tears or anger or grumpiness. But it does mean there's a background knowing that all those experiences are okay and temporary and an inevitable part of life. It does mean that I don't try and get in there with hammer and wrenches to fix their apparent pipework problem.

Unconditional love is able to just be with what's happening without needing to change or fix – the experience of non-judgement we've all been searching for, and it was already here.

About Helen Amery
I help people who are disillusioned with life to reconnect to this innate brilliance that we all are. We've all been sold a story about happiness lying at the end of an education, a good job, a family, house and car – and then we get there and wonder why all the hard work hasn't paid off. We still feel unfulfilled, insecure, unhappy. All because we've been taught to find happiness where it never existed. If you'd like to learn more, go to my website www.wildfigsolutions.co.uk – it has free resources and links to all the social channels you can connect with me on.

Sheela Masand

"Love and understanding harmonize the mind of humanity to its true inner nature."
Syd Banks - The Missing Link

I woke up on my 56th birthday in a chair at the side of my beautiful 26 year old daughter who was lying in a hospital bed. Less than 24 hours had passed since I had gone through the intense pain and anxiety of wondering whether I would lose her forever. Losing a child is something no Mother ever, ever wants to experience. I am very fortunate that did not happen and very grateful indeed.

I wasn't allowed to be with her the previous day and had no choice but to go home and wait for news while she was going through the tests alone. I felt totally powerless. Every cell of my body was crying out to do something to help my baby girl and there was nothing I could do. When she finally called to break the news to me, I howled like an animal hardly able to relay the news to her sister through the sobs and breathlessness.

The unwelcome news was a diagnosis of 3 intra-abdominal abscesses due to a complication of Crohn's disease and if they burst she could die of septicaemia. No doctor actually voiced the word "die" to us, but we all understood the severity of the situation especially given the urgency of her consultant in running tests and ordering procedures.

This wasn't the first time I thought I had lost my youngest daughter. When she was a tiny 2 month bundle of joy she stopped breathing and went as rigid as a board after I followed doctor's instructions to clear her nasal mucus with a syringe.

I went into a sheer panic and screamed at my husband to do something. Fortunately it wasn't many seconds before she came around again, but those seconds felt eternal and I suffered for a long time after that. I blamed myself for not only using the syringe, but for the panic and non-action on my part. I tortured myself through recreating the scenario in my head of what could have happened if my husband hadn't been there.

Although the description of my two unfortunate experiences sound very similar, I am very grateful to say that by the time my daughter was an adult I had come to see that who we are is not who we think we are.

In the second experience even while I was lying on my bed full of angst, there was a deeper quiet knowing that the essence of who she truly is cannot be lost and will be around forever.

It was a moment in time that illuminated how much my world has changed through realising the true nature of us all. With hindsight I can see the true impact of understanding even a tiny slither of the timeless infinite well of potential that is our true nature.

I know for sure that we are not who we think we are ie, the ever changing ideas, the beliefs, the labels, the judgements, the self-image and the body.

We are that which never changes.

If I hadn't realised the truth of that statement, I would have been absolutely wrecked and not nearly as present as I was during the 4 weeks' of hospital stay, treatments, tests and more sleeping in the chair. In fact, I imagine I wouldn't have slept very much at all.

There was a time when resilience was something I had to create or work on, somewhere to get to and something to maintain. Now I see that resilience is innate. It's where we land when we stop trying to make it happen and stop looking for it because it's ever present. It's what we are made of. I knew that my daughter has resilience and that I have it too along with the rest of the family. I knew we could be OK whatever the journey ahead of us and we have been.

When I first came across the idea of our true nature or consciousness or innate health (choose your label), it felt like a good idea or something to believe in, but not something I knew for sure. I may have been one of the slow learners! But it's not something we learn, it's something that is revealed or uncovered through insight. It took me several years of "staying in the conversation" before I could say I knew without a shadow of a doubt that there is (please forgive my clumsy words pointing to something invisible and all pervasive that cannot be explained) an eternal loving formless energy of which we are made and constantly dance in and out of with little or no awareness.

We are love. We are peace. We are wisdom. And infinitely more that words can only point to.

About Sheela Masand
Sheela Masand is an international coach, mentor and event organiser, helping people live happier, healthier lives.
Her mission is to raise the consciousness of humanity in order to prevent atrocity in the world. She sees this as a ripple effect. As each human being awakens to how experience is created from within and the magnificence of who they truly are, there will be no reason to for any type of destructive behaviour.

You can find out more about how she helps in the world of business too on her website: www.sheelamasand.com. Contact her directly on email: Sheela@sheelamasand.com

Claudette Dietlin

"God I am, but I am not God."
Attributed to Sydney Banks

True nature, essence, essential nature – words used to point to that formless, pure, spiritual something at the very core of everything that is alive. We can't see it. It isn't a thing that has form, but rather an aspect of something. Some say true nature is another word for God.

God. Not the God of my childhood – a deity demanding perfection and who sat in judgment of what I said, did, and thought. An entity who decided what prayers got answered and what prayers went unanswered. Who was chosen and who was not. No, not this God. Rather, the God I've come to know through my own exploration. That part of me I came into this world being, that part of me that never changes, that part of me where an intelligence wiser and deeper than my intellect resides. This God. The God inside me.

This God I know by feel. It seems I experience my true nature – the God within me when I feel open rather than closed, expansive rather than shut down, alive rather than deadened or numb. When I feel congruent and aligned with the deeper intelligence in me that knows without knowing how it knows. It just knows. It knows what to do. It knows when to do it. This just-in-time intelligence that is responsive to what arises as it arises. This force that lives me moment by moment throughout my life.

That my true nature is God feels true to me. God is the spiritual part of me that animates the human part of me. We are both formless and form – spiritual and human. Spiritual beings having a human experience, as it is often said.

Another name for God is Love. Love that has no limits or conditions. Unconditional love. I get glimpses of this and moments when I experience it. Love without conditions. I'm not a parent, but I imagine this is what a mother or father feels when they first look into the eyes of their newborn baby. Unconditional love. Undeserved in the usual sense of the word. But deserved beyond measure just because she or he is. This child is here, in this world. Invited or not by human terms, but unequivocally welcomed and whose arrival is celebrated in the spiritual realm. How could God not welcome and celebrate the arrival of itself in form?

I have only moments of experiencing what feels like unconditional love. Glimpses into what feels boundless, limitless and beautiful, beyond words. I suspect this is what God/Life sees as ordinary and we experience only in moments when our consciousness raises to a level where we catch a glimpse and experience a feeling of love for which we have no words and that has no boundaries.

Sydney Banks' words, "God I am but I am not God" ring true for me. There are times when I know this truth deep in my bones. I grew up believing I was on my own. The saying, "If it is to be, it is up to me" looked true. Believing this to be how life works, most of my time and energy went into manipulating circumstances on the outside so I could feel safe on the inside. It never worked. No matter how hard I tried, no matter what strategies I thought of and employed, I didn't experience the feeling of security and peace of mind I knew, at some level, were possible. It wasn't until I was pointed to look in the direction of the deeper intelligence that exists in all of us, to look inside rather than outside that I began to see how Life really works. We are God in human form. We are all connected to the One Source of all life. Our experience of life comes from the inside – that is where we experience what we call reality. The world of form and circumstances are continually changing and shifting. But what's inside of us – our true nature, is unchangeable. Unbreakable. Cannot be damaged. This is what I know to be true. This is what I can count on. It has made all the difference.

I bring a lifetime of curiosity and exploration of the human experience to my work as a coach. I also bring a lifetime of seeking, in both the psychological and spiritual realms, for principles I could rely on. It wasn't until I came across the 3 Principles that I found the solid ground I was looking for – principles in which there are no exceptions. From this place, I help people see they have everything inside of them, right now, to live life more fully and experience more aliveness. When people get even a glimpse of their potential, their experience of life changes - first on the inside and then on the outside. I know this because this has been my experience and I've seen it with virtually every client I've worked with.

As a coach, I help people rediscover who they are at their core - their true nature. Some describe this as the experience of coming home. I point people back to that deeper place that exists in all of us. That wise place inside us that sometimes seems so ordinary we miss it. But we've all had the experience of just knowing, even when we don't know how we know that we know. This is our built in GPS system and we can use it to navigate life, no matter our life's journey.

About Claudette Dietlin
I'm a graduate and Certified Transformative Coach from Michael Neill's Supercoach Academy and Amy Johnson's Change Coach program. I obtained a master's degree in Counseling Psychology from Antioch University. My personal work includes Authentic Movement, Depth Psychology, and a 30-year writing practice.

Clare Dimond

"Reality is an illusion, albeit a persistent one."
Albert Einstein

What would you love the world to know about true nature
and unconditional love?

It's an interesting question because the more our true nature
of unconditional love is realised, the less conditions there are
on anything in the world. It becomes clear that the world
appears at the same time as the idea of self, made of the
same conditioned thought.

The appearance of the world as a separate, objective truth is
a misunderstanding and the inevitable suffering points out the
confusion.

The appearance of the world as the miracle of life in apparent,
transient form is simply unconditional love seeing itself.

So, we could say that there is nothing the world needs to
know. As Gandhi said, 'Be the change you wish to see in the
world'. It is only here for something different to be realised. It
is only here for confusion to fall away and reveal that there is
no one to make any changes and no one to be changed.

Then there are words, actions, moving out into form and an
unconditional intimacy with the world.

How has this deeper seeing changed your world?

Another interesting question because the first thing that
happens is that the world does literally become 'your' world.

The whole world, all people, events, animals, everything arise within this space that we are.

And the effect of this is, ironically - considering we are talking about no objective reality - a greater immersion in the world of form and perhaps a greater accountability for it.

I've found that as old ideas of who I am and what I need fall away, there is absolute simplicity. There is the next thing to do, the next thing to be said or to write with not much sense of anyone deciding. And the old suffering which used to be a fast-track back to the trying and exhaustion is now just a beautiful indication of confusion.

There have been apparent 'external' changes in my life. My husband and I have divorced. My work is moving into different areas. But actually, these are trivial changes because it's become clear that the form of things is never an indication of any truth. The truth, the knowing of unconditional love and the realisation when confusion veils it, is all there is.

About Clare Dimond
I spent decades trying to fix myself and to be at ease with who I was and literally tried every type of intervention. Now it is fascinating to see how the understanding of no objective reality plays out in the 'real' world. What happens to money or work or health or relationships or stress or anything else as the idea of self falls away?

Every other month I run an online course to either look at the nature of reality or to look at one of these areas to explore it more deeply through conversations and webinars. And often there is a short book that follows:

REAL, the inside-out guide to being yourself

FREE, the inside-out guide to life unlimited
EASE, the inside-out guide to getting real with work
GAME: getting real with the play of life
SANE, getting real with reality

All the programmes are available on www.claredimond.com

Gabriela Maldonado-Montano

"It is almost like you are shining a light on their divinity."
Marien Perez

Interview

What would you love the world to know about true nature and unconditional love?

I would like the world to know that looking in the direction of unconditional love allows us to have conversations that ignite our creativity, innovation and resilience. I would also like people to know that when we recognize and honor true nature in each other - in spite of our differences - we are better positioned to have dialogue that would ultimately help us reach harmony.

These two elements need to be at the center of personal conversations as well as solutions and interventions at a global level.

We often listen to each other from our opinions, likes, dislikes. We tend to connect to others based on whether we agree or disagree with their world view, we often forget people are not their ideas. We need to have conversations that go beyond our particular opinion or concepts about the world and about each other. There's a part of us that we share, we share our humanity, that's what we have in common. We all want to have a life of harmony, hope, joy and kindness for our loved ones and ourselves.

How has this deeper seeing changed your world?

SEEING has given me the opportunity to enjoy, value and appreciate friends, colleagues, and family members that have a different world view than I have. It allows me to remember that I can deeply love other people even when I think differently from them, have different values, or life experiences. It allows me to honor their essence and not get confused thinking that just because they see the world different from me, we are at odds. It allows me to listen to others with a genuine desire to understand and not to judge.

I have lots of loved ones that have different world views, politics, and beliefs, than I. Some of them have opposite opinions than I do, fortunately for me, realizing true nature in all of us has given me the opportunity to experience unconditional love.

About Gabriela Maldonado Montano
Gabriela Maldonado Montano has dedicated her entire professional life to help her clients discover the wellbeing and natural genius that resides at the center of human beings. In over two decades of sharing the fundamental laws that create the human experience, she has worked individually and in groups across many settings including; education, alcohol and drug recovery, youth and adult incarceration, community development, burn out prevention, and executive coaching. Seeing her clients blossom regardless of the particular culture, gender, age or circumstance inspires her to continue her work in English and Spanish across this awesome world.

Gabriela had the incredible opportunity of being part of organizations at the forefront of change such as the Santa Clara County Department of Alcohol and Drug Services and the Center for Sustainable Change both in the USA. Both organizations strengthen her commitment to serve people in the most severe of circumstances. She has been honored to provide services alongside many coaches, trainers, and training organizations nationally and internationally.

Today Gabriela lives alongside her lovely husband Wil and her adopted cat Honey in Gilroy, California. She is profoundly grateful for the partnerships she has across continents that allow her to discover the innate creativity and resourcefulness in herself and others. Gabriela has found a renewed commitment to share a simple understanding that allows her to live with a sense of infinite possibilities.

Ilona Ciuanaite

"Out beyond ideas of wrongdoing
and rightdoing there is a field.
I'll meet you there.

When the soul lies down in that grass
the world is too full to talk about.

Ideas, language, even the phrase each other, doesn't make
any sense."
Rumi

What would you love the world to know about true nature and unconditional love?

Not knowing what you are is the root of all suffering. Knowing what you are dispels illusions and you are at peace.

We are born into this life and we are given a name. We grow and learn from parents and people around and we don't know any better than to believe what they say to be the truth of how things are.

As innocent children we take beliefs in of those around us and build our understanding of the world based on that. Years and years later we find ourselves in the position, where life seems to not work, there is a sense that this is not enough, there must be more to life and that sense brings us to the point of wanting to find out the truth. If you are lucky. Not everyone gets that call. But if you do, if you have enough of life that feels incomplete and somehow not working, you start questioning your beliefs and you find out that none of them are yours.

155

Then comes a time to raise a question- who am I? What am I? And a spiritual search begins. This is an individual process and no one else can answer those questions but you. There are many teachers, gurus, advisors, psychologists, life coaches who will give you their version of who you are and if you take their words to be the answer you stay stuck in the illusion believing what other people say. The only way out is to find out for yourself, for the love of truth.

Your natural state is always here. Like water in a lake, when there is no wind, it is still, there are no waves, it is deep and peaceful. So is the natural state, there is peace, stillness, spaciousness underneath all happenings, underneath all stories and emotions. Here now, there is beingness. Simply know that you are, you are here, now, present and aware. This can be recognised. And once this deeper peace of being is recognised, you can come here often and rest, leaving all the worries, burdens, and turbulence behind, allowing grace to take care of them.

Resting in peace is like a new dimension of human experience. A place within is found and a refuge can be taken. And from here the unconditional love arises. Love that knows no limitation, no judgements and no categories. It's love of being, love of knowing yourself as natural, relaxed, open being.

It is possible to live a life of peace, calmness, openness, playfulness and contentment. But to get there one needs to want to find out the truth of one's true nature, one needs patience and willingness to meet everything that arises, everything that is perceived as an obstacle to inner peace. It takes time. This process can be very intense, but it's necessary. And it's up to an individual. It's up to you to find peace and love that is always here, ready to be expressed.

The heart wants to love, it wants to send and receive love freely. If it is not able to, there is longing for that love that comes from a very deep place within. The longing is calling you to answer it, to be with it. But our minds are uncomfortable with the longing and are looking for ways to extinguish it, or at least to put it on hold, so that the call of the longing is no longer bothersome. And so we live life trying to avoid uncomfortable feelings, running away to the next thing that promises an escape. The mind cannot understand that the way to satisfy the longing is through meeting it fully.

Once you stop running from yourself, from the feeling that arises when you sit still, in silence, once you are ready to allow the longing to bring you home, magic happens. The longing for love meets with your attention and dissolves into love. This is grace. This is surrender. This is when the heart is set free and it loves it.

If you know this, you can meet the longing and let it guide you into your heart, where all is well. And here you can rest and recharge, allowing the love to nourish you, filling up the whole being. Words can't describe this. It is felt as openness and sweetness, as an energy fountain coming out of your chest into the world. I wish for everyone to find this place of inner spaciousness and live life in harmony, balance and love.

How has this deeper seeing changed your world?

My world before seeing one reality was painful. I believed thoughts about how life is not enough, how I was trapped and I could find no exit from a limited form. Inside I felt frustrated, incomplete and confused.

On the outside my life was normal, I had a great job, doing tattoos, meeting people from all over the world. I had lots of fun working as a tattoo artist in Brighton, England.

My life was filled with normal ups and downs, normal everyday sorrows, regrets, guilt, blame, worries and fears. I was full of wanting to achieve, to become, to be the best, to understand, to change and fix others. I wanted to know why people suffer and how to help them and I did not know how. That hurt.

After finishing school I went to study psychology, thinking that I will find the answers to my questions about the mind and how it works. I was curious and fascinated by the mind and its abilities. And I also wanted to learn how to help people to solve mental and emotional problems. But the knowledge that I received at the university did not give me the answers. I felt I learned about many theories, but the practical side was not touched. The thirst to find the key to undo suffering remained active in me for years.

My real seeking for the truth began in the early two thousands. It was a wet November in England, seasonal darkness was settling in. I and my partner lived in Brighton, in a tiny one-bedroom apartment. A friend came to visit and gave us a gift- a little bag of magic mushrooms. We took them and it was incredible. I have experienced what I never thought possible- silence of the mind. There were no thoughts coming, that seemed like for hours. I was sitting in a candle lit room, listening to music, being. Simply being. It felt like home. This was so sweet and free. That experience has opened the door to knowing that reality is not what it seems, that there is being, underneath all thinking, emotions and appearances. I have received the gift of knowing beingness, that felt like being at home, within myself.

That trip was profoundly beautiful, and it changed the way I looked at life. Now it seemed that I had to find that peaceful spacious place in me again and so my search began. I knew that there must be an access to simply being without taking anything.

It took me eight years to find the answer. It was hiding in the most unexpected question - is there an Ilona running the show?

This question came in, the mind stopped. There was a little gap. There was seeing that no one was there, and recognition happened. There is no Ilona as an entity, that is separate from the whole and there never was.

All is one reality appearing as many.

My world view shifted dramatically. Everything looked fresh. The old belief system centred around me, the character started to crumble and lose its solidity.

Even though the shift was subtle and almost unnoticeable, the outcome was a dramatic change. With realising unity, non-separateness of life, many worries, griefs, stories about the past and fantasies about the future fell away. It seemed as if an amusement park opened in my mind and I got an invitation to take new rides. I had many insights; many resolutions and many beliefs fell off. At the same time new, fresh understanding and seeing life differently was settling in. It felt exhilarating and liberating. I was so amazed by the experience that I felt I had to let everyone know how to find being.

Now I finally knew how to help others to end the search and find peace within. The way out of suffering was through knowing the difference between real and imaginary.

Externally my life changed as well. After working for many years in a tattoo shop, I had the courage and trust in myself to open up our own shop. We moved to a different town to start our own business. That felt like freedom. I could enjoy my own space, doing tattoos that I wanted to do, living in a quiet place, close to the sea. I felt blessed.

Immediately I started to write a blog and share with readers about this newfound freedom. Many people contacted me, and I guided them to realisation. In 2011 the Liberation Unleashed (LU) website and forum was born, out of love for humanity and being of service. It began with only a few of us, but we had enough fire to create something amazing - an online community of guides, who can point to realisation by asking questions. All this is free of charge.

My world now was filled with service. I was guiding in the forum and over email, holding live meetings, writing books, creating Liberation Unleashed structure, and talking to a lot of people. In the daytime I was doing tattoos, in the evenings I was making waves, inviting people to discover the selfless nature in their own experience.

Many people have joined LU forum. Currently, there are around seven and a half thousand members, with almost two and a half thousand conversations that ended in realisation.

Ten years later I feel relaxed in life, trusting that all is well, that there is no need to worry. I no longer feel regret, shame, guilt, blame and even though I can get annoyed at some trivial stuff, this feeling passes away quickly. I am no longer feeling stuck, limited or in a prison of my own making. I am feeling the joy of being and inner freedom. It took some intense undoing and sometimes I felt like I was going through hell. I experienced the highest high and the lowest low, that I never imagined possible. Differently from before now there was openness to feel, willingness and ability to meet life's challenges and more spaciousness to rest as being. Even in the middle of a storm I could feel stillness. Many storms came and went, life continuously brings new challenges and opportunities to learn, to surrender, to include all.

My process of transformation is taking many years. It wasn't one look and healing happened. It took patience, trust and surrender to life. When all the fighting with life ceases, there is a sense of flow - all is well right here right now.

With awakening to one reality came a lot of challenges and new adventures. Seeing that there is no separate self, gave space to allow all that is happening to pass by easier, with less resistance. I would say that it is a very intense process and all wounds and old beliefs come up. If they are met they can release and so more peace is felt within.

About Ilona Ciuanaite

These days of summer 2020 I'm living in Lithuania. Just me and my husband. Our house is at the edge of a little town, by a small forest and green fields. It's lovely and peaceful here. I can see a lot of sky, listen to birds and crickets.

I work with people over Skype, individually and with groups. I no longer do tattoos, as all my energy is focused on assisting people to find inner peace. I love witnessing a transformation and this keeps me inspired to continuously share.

I enjoy making YouTube videos. It's something new for me and there is so much to learn, it's challenging and makes me grow. So, my days are filled with ordinary living, enjoying what life gives, working with clients from all over the world, some writing, interviews, a lot of learning and creating.

I like to watch YouTube videos, an occasional series, I love cooking and making new dishes.

I love life and enjoy seeing magic underneath all appearances.

It's such a mystery. And wonder. Hope you can see this too!

www.liberationunleashed.com

Claire Shutes

When asked, "Are you a god or a man?" The Buddha replied, "I am awake."

What would you love the world to know about true nature and unconditional love?

Our essential nature is unconditional love.
A space of truth and knowing.
Connection. Acceptance.
Healing. Regeneration.
Wholeness.
Oneness.
Understanding beyond logic.
The simple question: "What more is there to see?"
Opens our hearts & minds when we have fallen into the illusion of separation.
Thought created illusion is the game of life.
Wisdom taps us on the shoulder calling us home.
Back to unconditional love.

How has this deeper seeing changed your world?

Knowing this to be true:
I feel connected to everyone.
I live in deeper feelings of love, peace & gratitude.
I am less reactive and more responsive.
I listen more.
I worry less.
I feel comfortable in the unknown.
I know whatever happens I will find a way through.
I cannot be broken.
I feel held and part of something bigger than me.

I recognise the god in all beings.
Until I don't.
When what I know becomes obscured.
Thank goodness what has been truly seen can never be forgotten.
I wake up again and again and again.

Claire Shutes
Master Transformative Coach

Denise Holland

"If we can get together and help the youth see the simplicity of life, see that they have this beauty inside of them, to see they have this power within them, the youth will grow up very very wise, and this world will change and become a far far better place to live in."
Sydney Banks

Who and What is Performing?

We are aware, all human beings have a mind, through which we get to experience life, we perceive, believe, discern, learn and develop. Through your physical bodies and minds, which grow, expand, age and then die, we get to see, touch, sense, hear and feel. It's a phenomenon beyond anything we can comprehend, yet many of us take it all for granted and do not make the leap to glimpse what it's all about profoundly.

I would love every living being to understand what and who we are at our core. How is it our heart beats, lungs breath and food digests all by itself? What is it that gives our minds the capacity to think, create or Be? In this material world of form, we have advanced in all areas of science, biology, chemistry and physics. Yet, we still haven't figured out how to collectively and collaboratively live in these bodies and minds, one species, living on planet earth together in peace and harmony. Finding out the true nature of human life would, in my mind, manifest the solution and create a world of unity, love and compassion as well as exploration and advancement.

As a national athlete and coach at the elite end of sports for over 30 years, I frequently crossed the line of say two worlds;

the personal and impersonal, which can be explained better in the question of who and what is performing? There are times when you strive, grind out your training, it hurts, you persevere, believing that you will be better when you achieve the goal. Then, without warning, you slip into another dimension of sport. It's not about you and the ideas you have about yourself and what it is you think you need to be okay, something else takes over. You become an explorer of human performance, riding the wave of existence, seeing what's possible through your body and mind, knowing nothing is lacking, competing feels light, even effortless at times.

Sensing that there is something else going on here, other than the material, physical and personal and taking action to delve deeper is probably one of the most significant awakening moments of my life. You wouldn't own a car and not know how it works; fill it with petrol, water for a clean windscreen, tyres with tread to keep it on the road, so why do we expect to navigate life without understanding what life is? It doesn't make sense to me!

Following the subtle calls, the voice of intuition and instinct to find out more about my true nature, who or what is behind human life has transformed the way I live in this body and mind. When I look for the anxiety and concerns which occupied my mind for so long around, doing well, being impressive, getting results, the feelings are no-where, where did they go? I didn't work on them, re-frame or rationalise them they dissolved all by themselves. From time to time, they re-visit, and for a while, I take them seriously hooked again in the material, personal world. Then, with insight, I remember the truth about human existence and how it works; there is a deeper intelligence; life is not all that it seems. The possibility of an illusory reality brings me back into Presence and peace.

In my parenting, I flit in and out of dimensions. In one moment, I experience stress about, am I doing enough to help and guide my children who are young adults now, especially when I can see them suffering. Then, it shifts, and I know that wisdom is not just guiding their lives, but is the core of their existence, creating ever-changing forms even the ones we don't like! I realise life doesn't happen in my timeframe. If I didn't have a sense of our true nature, I would live in suffering way more of the time, my living minutes hijacked by temporary, insecure thinking that looks solid and real to me at the time.

Seeing beyond our illusory realities that have us stuck in old habitual beliefs releases us to experience our innate raw materials of being human, wellbeing, resilience, gratitude, and heaps of creativity. I find myself devoted to this cause, freeing people's minds to create a more sustainable, loving, united world.

About Denise Holland

My career as a coach in elite sports performance for over 20 years, fuels my continuous exploration into what a person is capable of achieving through the physical body and mind.

As the captain of the national Hong Kong netball team, I know all about the highs, lows and struggles that go with the territory of success, failure and results! After two World Netball Championships as a player, I moved into coaching, working with two England Netball Super league teams.

As Scotland's performance director and national netball coach, I presided over the team's move up the world rankings to 12th place and qualification for the Commonwealth Games in 2014. What I came to realise is that physical prowess, superior skill capacity and exceptional game understanding, although excellent qualities do not produce world-class teams. For years, I was missing the ultimate game-changing performance variable, a persons' use of the human mind!

As a Human Performance and Wellbeing consultant, I help people to understand the power of the mind, that they live and perform freely, without judgement and beliefs which hinder their enjoyment and results. It seems vital to me to go upstream and help people to profoundly understand the source of all human endeavour, as a way of resolving conflict, improve leadership, manage difference and enhance performance.

www.class-performance.com
www.twitter.com/Denise_Holland
www.facebook.com/DeniseHolland3Ps

Piers Thurston

*"What we need in the world now more than ever, is to realise
a fresh understanding about what we truly are (pure love,
and the unconditional nature of Source) and what appears to
turn up to us psychologically, in our perceptual realities
moment to moment."*
Piers Thurston

Audio transcription

What would you love the world to know about true nature and
unconditional love?

Unconditional love and true nature are not really things you
can talk about! What I can do with words is just point using a
language map, but there is something that is much more than
any words. Having said that, given that's all we've got, let me
have a go with words...

What I'm talking about here is not the same as personal love
or intimate love that you might experience romantically or
even love between a parent and a child. Those things are all,
from love and made of love. For me true love is another way
of describing what is at the very foundation; it is source, it is
consciousness, it pre or before everything. It's the bridge
between the 'allness' and the 'isness'. It's the very fabric of
what we are. In saying what we are, I don't mean me the
separate self, you the separate self, I mean the thing that
creates that.

What's useful to know about true love? That it is totally
universal and non-discriminate to who you are or who you
think you are. It's not that some people have it, and some
people don't, we are made of the stuff, it's pre that. When we

experience it in a purer form, with less conditional conceptual narrative and less me, then it turns up as a pure sense of peace, bliss, connection and awe. People have probably had glimpses of that in their lives.

It's what I am pointing people to with this work, to see that and feel that more. Many people have had experiences of true love and can listen to the songs about it or the poetry about it or the spiritual talking about it. I think that what we need in the world is to know what relationship there is between that pure source love, unconditional nature and what turns up to us psychologically, in our perceptual realities moment to moment.

The other useful thing to know is that often it doesn't look like that love is there, but that despite this, we are true love. There are many people who believe that they don't have it. That doesn't mean it is true, that's just the narrative that someone has put in their life. What I'm pointing people to see is that whatever has happened to you in your life, to date, is irrelevant to you exploring true love now. This is because this is something that has nothing to do with the content of our personal reality. This has nothing to do with what turns up for us on the surface of the waves. This is something underneath, much deeper.

It seems to be that the more someone insightfully understands that this is something 'beyond or before psychology', the more they spend their time nearer to that love, the wonderfulness of that love, the intelligence, the innate compassion, resilience, clarity, connection and inspiration. When someone looks in this direction or touches that space, with more of an absence of the conditioned self, they seem to experience more of it. And that realisation is incredibly useful too because it means that we don't get so weighed down by what turns up for us psychologically. We don't buy into the ego's claim that it's our job to sort that psychological stuff out. We have more ease with life we are in flow, we are more graceful with the lows and grateful for the highs.

In the last few hundred years humans have been so interested, fascinated and educated in what the conceptual mind brings to the party that we've ignored what's behind that, before that, beneath that, within that, because it's too intangible for the conceptual separate self us to understand. Therefore, in society it gets left in a very amorphous, ineffable place for spiritual people to look at. I believe what we need to do is to help people see the ordinary nature of it, and once seen, people often experience life with more ease and flow.

To understand this more is about where to look, but you can't see true love, it is impossible because once you've seen it, you're an entity in it. You are made of it, you can't see what you're made of. So instead, I point people to where not to look, as most of us have been conditioned to look to the content of the experience, attributing experience or reality to things in form, and including the self in that. So instead, the more we look to the direction of the nature of the system - and how it ebbs and flows rather than to try and fix our psychology through either changing the world, the environment, the situation, the past and the future, the more aligned with any emergent reality in the moment we are. Exploring the nature of experience, as opposed to the content of it, that's the bit that we're missing.

How has this deeper seeing changed your life?

Well, probably similar to lots of other people but it's funny, I can't actually remember what it was like not to know this. But I think what I would say is that there is so much more ease and flow with what happens and less expectation that I need to fix things. I know I'm not psychologically in charge of what's going on so there's less burden on me to be or do. I'm involved, I'm the custodian of my experience, but I don't need to stress or burden myself in trying to work out things I don't know. I know something will emerge and I know that I'm okay no matter what at the level that matters.

Whatever happens to me in form, in life, I know I have an innate capacity for joy, connection, love and inspiration. Nothing, nothing, nothing, nothing, can take that away, it's impossible, it's just not how the system is designed. Now I might have preferences on how I want the world to be or how I want me to be, but that's not going to take away those innate attributes at the level that matters. That's a wonderful thing to know. I don't have to work life out I know I'm okay. There's so much more flow, there's such a wonderful potential for awe and inspiration in anything. It can be as simple as walking outside and looking at the sunset. You don't have to do anything amazing to get it. You're not on some ladder or rat race or hamster wheel.

In terms of how that's turned up for me in life, I've dedicated my work to this now. I was always in the coaching world, but this understanding has completely changed how I go about my work. It has helped me in my parenting, in my relationships, it's helped me in everything really. I'm so grateful that this is what I've stumbled across. I can't imagine not knowing this now, it's wonderful!

About Piers Thurston
Piers is a coach working with businesses internationally. You can find details on his website www.qualityofmind.biz or www.piersthurston.com. Also he has a podcast series on www.qualityofmind.co.uk and a YouTube channel www.youtube.com/c/qualityofmind

Damian Mark Smith

*"It is not that we have a short time to live,
but that we waste a lot of it."*
Seneca

Interview

What would you love the world to know about true nature and unconditional love?

It's all about simplicity for me. When you see that our experience is created internally by us or you could say created internally by some sort of energy that comes through us. And you know that we are alive, we think, and we feel our thinking that's a game changer. It's a game changer because we can stop blaming the outside world.

Now when it comes to being or connecting with that intelligent energy, it has a bit of a track record. It does some cool stuff like builds universes. I heard recently that there's something like 40 new galaxies every second being created out there in the universe, it is mind blowing, isn't it? It's such a creative universe!

And we spend so much time in lack when, the creative force is out there. It is summer here in the UK and nature is expanding and it's growing and that to me is the tapping into universal love, which is just the creative force. And we are that because every single time we have a thought, it's that creativity which is exploding in our brains. And that's what's happening. We are exploding in that creativity.

But we don't see it, we don't know it, we don't experience it. We don't even know it's happening. We just put our heads down and trot along with the day not really tapping into the fact that there's this incredible energy creating through us in every minute of every day. And we are full of potential, that potential of the creative universe is coming through us.

And we can test that it's true, we can see it, we can feel it. If you want to know what a miracle is go and look in the mirror. But we forget, you know, we get caught up in the bills and the kids, if we're lucky. Most living creatures in the universe, as far as we know, don't have that option. A second is a very long time for a Mayfly, which appears one day every two or three years. It appears, it mates and then it dies. That's it, it's gone. Every second is precious for that Mayfly. We don't really experience that. The problem with most humans is that we don't remember things, not because we don't have good memories, but because we would never present in the first place. If you ask people what they were doing this time last week they probably can't remember. It's because they were thinking about the future or thinking about the past, but they weren't in the present. And the issue is not that life is short it is that we waste so much of it.

When we tap into that creative force when we are present in that moment, miracles await. And that's what I do, I point people back to that. I help people to get present and there are many ways of doing that because we are presence. I also help them to tap into that creative freedom that's available. People come to me with problems, and I show them that they already have the solution. And they're very thankful for that.

How has this deeper seeing change your world?

In simple ways. I used to have acute OCD and I'd really struggle to function on a daily basis. I had stress, depression,

174

anxiety, and all sorts of stuff. And nowadays, I just have thinking, which I ignore. Not every day, I don't choose to ignore it every time. But mostly I look at it and I see it for what it is, as opposed to it being something that controls me and makes me do stuff. You know, life can't make you think about it. And your thinking can't make you do something with it. Well, that's kind of useful to know!

Why don't they teach that in psychology school? It has been life changing for me to know I don't have to pay attention to thinking. I don't need to dwell on it, work out where it came from or try to stop it. Not paying attention to my thinking, especially when it's going off on one, that's been useful to know. Also tapping into it when it is useful. Our useful ideas come from the infinite potential of the universe.

I have an easier life but only because I made it difficult beforehand. It wasn't that an easy life wasn't there, but it was covered up by me making it a difficult life. Silence is here, it's hiding in plain sight, it's just covered with all the noise. The silence doesn't go away, when you take the noise away, you're left with the silence. It is the same with an easy life, it's the same with an effortless life, it's there anyway, we just make it hard for ourselves. We spend all of our time thinking it's supposed to be hard. When, I think it's supposed to be easy.

About Damian Mark Smith

I mainly coach entrepreneurs, helping them with their businesses. Looking at strategies behind their businesses and the thinking behind the strategies behind their businesses. If someone is stuck, the problem is not keeping them stuck. It's their thinking about the problem that keeping them stuck. And it's their thinking you might say is the only thing that's keeping them stuck. The next question usually comes in, well, how can I make it change? The bad news is you can't make it change. But the good news is, is going to change anyway. You don't have to do the heavy lifting because the heavy lifting is done for you. That's, the beauty of the system. That's the love behind the system. It's designed to change. And the more we try and do it ourselves, it's like a bad DIY person the more they do the worse it gets. We can let the experts do it, the experts in this case is new thought. The way to access that is we let go. When we let go of the need, when we let go of the thinking about the thinking. When we let go of the I have to change this. When we let go of the I have to solve this. New thought can come along.

rethinkingbusiness.biz
human-ios.com
damian@rethinkingbusiness.biz

David Key

*"No matter how far down the wrong road you've travelled,
turn back."*
Turkish proverb

Audio Transcript

When I heard the quote above I never really understood why it meant so much to me. Later I understood the reason why. Around ten years ago, my world started to fall apart. My relationship almost went off a cliff, my wife and I were going in different directions. We had a few children, and I was extremely anxious. We were unhappy as a couple, and divorce was on the cards. I mean, most people from what was going on in our relationship would say, "There's no way those two will ever be together." Well, here we are over a decade later, and our relationship just keeps getting deeper and deeper. You could say that unconditional love is coming through, and what I hope for the world, what I'd love for the world to see is what we were so fortunate to be able to wake up to.

We woke up to the truth about human beings' true nature. As it happened to us, I know the potentiality of this understanding for seven billion people on the planet is exactly the same, and here's why. Here's what I see about unconditional love and our true nature. All human beings, it doesn't matter how tall, how short, male, female, whether you live on that side of the world or this side of the world, what you look like, what you sound like, what your life experiences are, that's just, for me, a simple description of the differences between human beings, from looking at the outside, "Oh, they're different from me," but here's where we're the same. You see, every single human being is made of energy, an invisible life force energy, an intelligent energy that has the power to get a heart working and keep up breathing. We don't have to think about all those things. That intelligence is built into life. If you look at nature and see the sunrise in the morning, and you see the leaves start to open up and absorb all the sunlight, and as the sun moves, the leaves follow the direction, or you see salmon swimming upstream to spawn, that intelligence is built into life.

It's also built into human beings because we're made of it. We are made of energy, and we're just in a different body suit. I'm sure, if all human beings could wake up to their true nature and see that energy, that life force energy is unconditional love life would be easier. We all feel it day-to-day, it's that beautiful feeling that washes over us when we see a baby, they're smiling at us and they exude unconditional love, and we can't help but get affected by that. We can notice all these lovely feelings when we see that.

That is unconditional love when we're not thinking about ourselves, and we're just seeing the beauty of an unconditioned child with no preconceived ideas about how the world works, how they should respond to human beings. They just see with pure innocence. I hope for the world that we can go back to that space that we were in when we came into this world, uncontaminated, no ideas about this or that, just in awe of the beauty - that's available to everybody.

I hope for the world that we wake up to the understanding that all human beings are experiencing an inside out reality. The world can't create your experience. I hope the world wakes up to the truth, that we're all the same, energy in a body suit, that all our feeling states are perfect. When we feel down, this intelligence is working perfectly. I hope human beings can see the connection between thoughts that they have that come into their mind and pass through, like the weather.

I hope human beings can wake up to the truth to say, "Those people out there couldn't possibly make me feel that way because all feeling states, love, hate, are coming from thought in the moment." I hope human beings can see there's no past and there's no future. We only have the present moment, the now.

If we could see that, then we would forgive because we would say, "There's no point in dwelling on the past because it doesn't even exist now, and going back into traumatic experiences or historical injustices, and then feeling bad about it isn't really the solution to a better world in my view. When human beings take responsibility for their own inside out understanding and if the world's seven billion people could wake up to that truth and see that they're made of unconditional love, that the only thing that can make us ever feel a certain way is what we're thinking in the moment, that could change the world. I wish for the world to wake up to the truth that human beings have a free will to use their thinking about the past and the future and thoughts in this illusory reality that we hypnotize ourselves with. I hope we can wake up to the fact that we can change that in a moment by seeing the truth, our true nature. That's what I hope for the world because it changed my world.

The other question was how has this deeper understanding, this deeper seeing changed my world?

It has changed my world, my wife's world, my children's world, going from a struggling relationship that wasn't looking too healthy to a loving relationship, where there was forgiveness. There was an opportunity to see that when we understand how the mind really works and the principles behind our experience, that we only ever feel what we're thinking. The thoughts that are coming through our minds, we don't have control over that, there's an intelligence there. If we could just learn to not be afraid of how we're feeling and what our experience is on the inside, I think the world would fall in love again.

For me, when every human being could look out into the world and see their feeling state isn't coming from out there, their feeling state is coming from inside. And all their judgments and all their holding onto the past, bad feelings, bad memories and experiences, just see that that's optional. You don't have to do that. That, for me, would change the world because we would forgive the people that harmed us, in the past, because we'd recognize that holding grudges and being scared of other human beings is a crazy idea because we could wake up to see we're all one. We're just this ball of energy. There is no difference between you, me, and anybody else on planet Earth. That's what I hope. I know it'll change the world if we could all wake up to the truth of our true nature.

About David Key

What am I up into the world - My company is called Auspicium Limited, or you could find me at DavidKey.com. I'm just doing my best to share the teachings of the theosopher and philosopher, Sydney Banks, who, in the 1970s, had an epiphany. He wasn't a psychologist or a people helper. He didn't ask for this to happen. He just had a realization of human beings having perfect mental health, innate health on the inside, like a perfect diamond. When the babies come into the world, uncontaminated by their thinking, all that happens is life experiences and thoughts cover the diamond, and it just becomes a ball of doo-doo, like a dung beetle we're trying to push it up a hill. If we could see the stuff that's covering the diamond is just made of thought and we can drop it at any time, then we'd do better in life.

Amir Karkouti

*"Life goes on, unconcerned whether interpretation
is present or absent."*
Vijai S. Shankar

I never thought I'd have the type of freedom I got the day I discovered that my penis might never work again. I remember the day so vividly. My wife was sitting on my right, and the prestigious Editor-in-Chief of The Journal of Sexual Medicine, world-famous urologist Dr Irwin Goldstein, was sitting in front of me with all his certificates and degrees plastered on the wall behind him.

Dr Goldstein is a straight shooter and got right down to business. The whole thing was fascinating from the outset. He was looking at my blood results and making faces as if he were inspecting a diamond. Finally, he looked up after what felt like forever and asked a simple question: "Have you ever taken Propecia, Amir?" I casually stated, "Oh, yeah, I took it for about six years but my wife got me to quit after she read that she could make deformed babies if she merely touched a pill." Turns out, I had innocently taken a pill that my general practitioner told me would reduce hair loss. I didn't think I was taking anything that could destroy my endocrine system.

What happened next only happens in movies...or to be precise, in horror films. Dr Goldstein slammed his fist on his desk and screamed out in his least professional voice, "F###!" His whole desk shook, and all the little medical trinkets and pens jumped as much as we did. My wife and I waited patiently for him to hopefully say, "Just kidding, you're gonna be fine..." But he didn't. Instead, he went on to say, "By your bloodwork, I knew something was up. Based on your hormone levels and your symptoms, you are a classic case of somebody who has 'crashed' from taking Finasteride, the generic version of Propecia. What this means is that I can probably fix all the stuff you're experiencing, like mental fatigue, muscle wasting, memory loss, anxiety, physical exhaustion, and so on. However, the last thing that tends to improve is erectile function. In other words, your penis might never work again. Amir, you are a classic case of what's called Post-Finasteride Syndrome."

My immediate response was, "Great, Doc! At least I know what's wrong." As happy as I was to hear that what I was experiencing could be diagnosed, a wave hit me right afterward that dissolved my momentary relief. I had thoughts about having children with my wife. How was that going to work out? I had thoughts about why a doctor would prescribe this shit to men, and darker thoughts of suing the disgusting pharmaceutical company for damaging a young man such as myself, and the thousands of other men who were probably going through this as well. But here's where it got interesting. I could see myriad thoughts passing by, and each of them had an emotion tied to it. I was literally in a maze of thought-feelings, going from feeling blessed to feeling like shit and back again. At that moment, I realized something. The circumstance had nothing to do with the thoughts that entered my mind.

In other words, the doctor told me a situation that had happened, and within five minutes I jumped onto a ride of emotions. No feeling had more validity than another. I couldn't pinpoint which emotion was truly tied to what the doctor had said. Dr Goldstein kept talking, and it started to sound like Kermit the Frog. He was going on about the treatment protocol, and it literally sounded like, "BLAH BLAH BLAH..." to me.

I was finally at peace. I knew Dr Goldstein had told me something that I "should" have felt bad about...but I didn't. Granted, bad feelings came and went, but so did good ones. And behind all that was racing through my mind, I saw the capacity I had to have any thought, at any moment, about any situation. I was free to experience thought taking form, moment by moment. And thought DID take form, regardless of what I was told. He could have said that I had peanut butter and jelly in my bloodwork, and I could have been angry, sad, jealous, excited (enter feeling here) or whatever Universal Thought was offering me. I saw it for the very first time. Thought was not related to the circumstance. The energy of Thought can show up with anything, and I will, by design, feel that thought. I saw the gift in action right before my eyes. I was in Heaven on Earth — not because of what the doctor said, but because I had a deeper feeling for who we are that was independent of what I had just heard.

My wife popped me out of this feeling of bliss when the doctor tried to get my attention. I think I came back to Earth about the third time the doctor said my name. "Amir...hey, Amir, are you OK? You seem a bit calm after the news I just sprang on you." I was still coming down from the high when my wife gently grabbed my knee and gave it a pat, and said, "Oh, Doc, I think Amir is too naïve to see this as a problem right now." I knew what she meant. Maybe she got a glimpse too. Who knows? I never asked. But what I heard when she said this was that I didn't see it as a problem at all. I saw it as a circumstance. I knew that, regardless of what the doctor said, the energy of Thought would make it seem like my feelings around what I had heard were coming from the doctor...but I saw it with my own eyes. I saw the different thoughts and feelings that passed through with the news. I didn't connect the circumstance with the feeling. Had I given it more thought than it needed, I would have believed that the circumstance made me feel the distress, anger, and frustration associated with the news I'd just received.

We will always experience an infinite level of feelings, no matter what circumstances arise. But for some reason, I knew at that moment that no feeling can ever be tied to a circumstance; it can only be tied to the thinking that shows up in the moment in spite of the circumstance. What I was experiencing wasn't simply the fact that my ding-a-ling might not work; I was feeling Thought flow through me, which was giving me the experience that I was angry at the circumstance. I was experiencing the energy of Thought taking form, independent of my circumstances. I thought about this for a minute. If I had been under anesthesia when the doc told me the news, I wouldn't have cared. I wouldn't have cared because there wouldn't be any thought to give it the experience.

I need the energy of Thought to experience the situation as good, bad, ugly, or terrifying. That was so surreal! And as strange as this may sound, I wouldn't trade the experience and "secret" I discovered during this brief encounter with my doctor for anything! OK fine, maybe I'd rather have had this experience getting ice cream or being gifted a new Tesla, but I'll take what I can get. And what I got was the Principles in action. What I got is what Sydney Banks so eloquently spoke about in his books and lectures. Strange as it may seem, I became a new man even though I lost a part of my manhood.

I guess many men might never understand this, but it's possible. I now volunteer for Dr Goldstein and speak to several patients a week who tell me that they are broken (or at least they think they are), that erectile dysfunction has ruined their lives and they will never be the same. I know one thing for sure: What I experienced is the Truth of our reality. It only works one way — from the inside out. So, having truth on my side helps when I speak to these men, who innocently believe that this circumstance has ruined them. I know that's impossible because as long as they have the capacity for fresh, new thought, the thought of them being ruined is just as fleeting as them seeing that they are not ruined. Alan Watts once said, "You are not obligated to be the same person you were five minutes ago." I would upgrade the quote to, "You are not obligated to believe the thought you had a moment ago." If you see your capacity, your God-given right to the Gift of Thought, moment to moment, then you are free from all circumstances. You are free from the shackles of the ups and downs of the energy of Thought. We are free to go beyond personal thinking, which can't influence our true nature behind thought. You are beyond all of it. You are not only beyond it, you are it!

You are the source from which all of it comes into creation. We forget that. I think we were designed to forget… After all, what fun would it be to always know our gifts? Then we wouldn't have human moments like this to write about. So, we get glimpses of what we are capable of. We get glimpses that our reality is made of Thought, yet Thought itself is not made of reality. We are the vessel that creation comes from. When you see it that way, there is no way that life can't be beautiful. I just wish somebody had told me this earlier.

About Amir Karkouti
Amir Karkouti is the author of five books including WTF Are the Three Principles. He worked at a recovery center in San Diego for four and a half years sharing the Three Principles as uncovered by Sydney Banks. You can find out more about Amir at www.amirkarkout.com.

Kimberley Hare

"Everything is either Love, or a cry for Love"

Marianne Williamson

When we think we love somebody or something, it is only ever our own Love we are experiencing.

Or, more accurately, universal Love, expressed through us.

I often reflect that the reason we are so obsessed in our culture with 'romantic love' (think pop songs, poems, romantic literature), is because this is the closest most of us come to experiencing that bigger love.

And there's nothing wrong with that – it's a wonderful gift.

But it's like a candle when compared to the brightness and warmth of the Sun.

We seek that warmth and brightness, that universal, infinite, unconditional Love, because it's what we're all made of.

We all want to come home to our true nature.

About Kimberley Hare
Kimberley Hare is a writer, transformative coach, facilitator and teacher of the Three Principles. You can find out more about her at www.heartofthriving.com

Julianne Del Cano-Kennard

"Understanding someone's suffering is the best gift you can give another person. Understanding is love's other name. If you don't understand, you can't love."
Thích Nhất Hạnh

"Compassion" and embracing the "Whole Self"

I feel it safe to say that we have all experienced love and the pain of losing love in ways that bring us to our knees.

It seemingly arrives on a vehicle of many forms. From the expiration of a loved one, to the silent, little-understood, 'deprivation' that is known only to you. It can be a clandestine 'truth' that is experienced so vividly within your own mind's narrative and irrefutably felt at depths only YOU can begin to disentangle.

What we must understand is the destination is very real and is the same for all, no matter the peerless form of its arrival. Pain is pain... but pain can also be a bitter-sweet yet exquisite doorway to a deeper understanding. This deep understanding brought forth not a finding of my "true self" but a re-acquaintance and full embracement of my "Whole Self". For me, pain was the delicately placed couloir to the "always known".

I will never forget the day my son was taken from me; In my eyes I was a failure. I was living within this perception of myself for quite some time. However, on this day, in my inner world, it was confirmed. An indescribable yet ferocious agony enveloped my entire physical form. An anguish so relentless and kinesthetically felt within the abysmal depths of my soul. My body lay motionless. An eclipse arose as every part of my outer world began to fall away. "I" was left floating in the darkness, "alone" in the silence.

However even deeper yet, a familiar knowing began to rise up and gently cradle my being. This non phonetic communication slowly grew stronger, closer, and even more familiar. Light emerged as my own intuitive essence began to permeate this silent, once dark space. While communing with the wildness of this intrinsic wisdom, an ever-growing understanding emerged that birthed a 'sublime love'. I call that 'sublime love' "Compassion" (love and understanding). I knew then, I was never alone --I knew then I was always "Whole". A new way of seeing began to surface that holds compassion for others but most importantly compassion for my own being, my "Whole Self".

This inner world of perception is alive in us all. It is unique and ever-changing. It directs us to shelter when we are cold, to get food when we feel hunger, and rest when we grow tired. It is the perpetual dance of our humanness that at times leaves a sense of feeling weary, lost and alone. However, it is also the uncovering of our own intuitive essence that rests in the hush of the present moment. It is the forever promenade of the 'unknown hand-in-hand with the always known'. It is our "Whole Self". Embracing our "Whole Self" means embracing the grittiness of life. It is the "grit" that births the smooth, just as sand on a beach births the beautiful, glass-like pebbles. It means moving forward not free from suffering, but embracing the suffering with freedom, with love, understanding and thus 'compassion'.

Julianne Del Cano Kennard
Innateevolution.com

Rudi Kennard

'The wound is the place where the Light enters you.'
Rumi

Note: I use the word 'God' in this writing. No disrespect but my version of 'God' is not religious but a universal interconnected power or force, and my personal 'felt' experience of this 'field' or essence is compassion or love. Love is poisonous to hate. But hate is not poisonous to love for hate is created in the mind of man, while love is what created the mind of man. One is created, the other is creation.

Hate created in the mind of man is held as long as it is thought, then as our thinking moves on it disappears until conjured into being by thought.

Love is not created in the mind of man, for it is the mind of God. It will be present regardless of what we think, and it cannot disappear for it has nothing to disappear into, apart from itself.

We give love form and meaning and say, 'love is this' or 'love is that'. As soon as we give something meaning it solidifies into form, and we believe the form of it rather than the power before the form. We have ideas of what love is, but the heart of God cannot be held in an idea, can we hold the ocean in a teacup? Love is beyond ideas. It can appear like a spacious remembering, gently blowing through the silence in your consciousness or it can appear cruel and unforgiving. But love just is, and is whatever we think 'it is', but love has no agenda, nothing to prove, nothing to get, no right and wrong, just the boundless manifestation of the un-manifest.

Lovingly smashing us down and at the same time lifting us up.

So, you may ask what is love? Maybe it is nothing you 'think' it is, but its timeless presence awaits you in its infinite embrace.

It awaits you on the edge of the universe, tirelessly patient, until the 'you' trying to observe it dissolves and then nothing to understand, there is just what is, then there is just home, a home that was never left.

I wrote this a number of years ago and although it is a piece of creative writing it is very real. I want to add a personal story to expand on what I wrote above to give the writing relevance in the 'everyday'.

Time travel back to 2015

I sat on the sofa looking up at my wife, she had just uttered the words 'I am in love with another man and this marriage is over'. The future that I had imagined in my mind disappeared as insubstantial as a ghost. My world collapsed. My heart split open as a tsunami of tears engulfed my cheeks.

I fell into a deep hole of pain so profound I could not see that she was in more pain than me uttering those few words. She walked out the door and that was the end of 'us'. She had tried to make 'us' work, but the 'them' (her and her new partner) was just perfect together- and still nearly six years later.

I sat alone on the sofa and a wall of the most dark and horrific feelings engulfed me and drew me down, down into an ocean of suffering. Then a curious thing happened. I asked God why is this happening to me? This was the answer:

'Because you asked for it!'

'I didn't ask for it!'
'You did ask for it. You asked to evolve, and this is evolution.'

Just then I remembered communing with this field and asking
'Please help me evolve so I could be of more service and
benefit to others'. It was a strong and powerful volition within
me as I asked, and I remember hearing an answer, although
I passed it off as my imagination at the time, saying 'are you
sure?', I said yes - no matter what.

I was stunned and sat in silence for a while then asked,
'I didn't ask not to have a relationship with my wife'.
'You will still have a relationship with her, just a different
one'.
'Is this actually God or just my imagination?'.

Just then there was a knock on the door. I ignored it but the
knock was persistent. Eventually I got up wiping my tears and
answered. I was presented with two men with pasted on
smiles who said:

'Do you believe in God?'

They were Jehovah Witnesses. I mumbled a reply then said
now was not a good time to talk. I think they could see
something was going on so one of them handed me a leaflet
and they said goodbye.

I walked back into the lounge and sat back on that sofa. I
looked at the leaflet and the title was 'God is with You.'

I sat stunned. I had asked and I had got an answer. God was
with me . . .

Travelling back to NOW 2020

I ended up meeting the most amazing woman in the universe, getting remarried, becoming a stepdad, living in Hawaii and being more blissfully in love than I ever thought possible. The voice in my mind had been right, the whole experience had evolved me, it had kindled a love within, not for a 'some-one' but for a 'someone-lessness'. It had uncovered a love within not attached to people or things but to a no-thing ness, the essence of what is. A pure, unfiltered, non-personal love. It is interesting as the subtitle of the leaflet was 'The Kingdom of heaven is within' I had been attaching my wellness to 'being' a someone, 'doing' a something and 'having' a someone. It was all based on impermanent 'things'. True permanent love is not in 'things' but a quiet remembering the majesty of the silence within. Then I get to do, be and have 'things' but with un-attachment to them making me feel like I feel.

It is amazing what happens as we 'de-thing' ourselves we don't need to please people, get people to like us, do things we think we 'should' do nor have to do a certain thing. When we stop acting, we remember we are not the role we are playing, we are not the screenplay we are featuring in, we are the writer of our own story, we are the creator of our own lives, we are the creator lovingly dancing. We are the heartbeat of the universe the celestial orchestra and each unique note is absolutely valued and needed to create the music of life. We are already whole, already loved, we are the perfect imperfection of the one essence.

I wanted to finish of with a quote from Rumi

'The wound is the place where the Light enters you.'

Let the light enter you, let the love get uncovered, live a life in love, it is the most beautiful life you can live. We will not be 'happy' all the time, but we will be truly human - anything apart from love is just a distraction.

Love and light Rudi Kennard

www.innateevolution.com

About the Author

Nicola Drew HG Dip.P is a qualified psychotherapist, coach and mindfulness teacher.. She helps clients gain clarity and freedom of mind to overcome unhelpful symptoms, behaviours and habits. She also works as a trauma specialist helping clients get relief from PTSD, working with trauma organisations such as PTSD Resolution and Red Poppy. Nicola works with individuals and organisations exploring wellbeing, mental health and state of mind. She has worked in a variety of settings such as schools, universities, prisons, with charities and with a number of businesses.

Nicola has a special interest in the deeper nature of the human potential. She believes that every person, no matter what their circumstances, has innate wellbeing which can be innocently veiled due to misunderstandings about who we really are and how life works. She enjoys guiding people on a more spiritual exploration of who and what they really are.

She lives in Leicestershire in the UK, but is originally from beautiful Northumberland.

To find out more about Nicola's work go to www.hippocoaching.co.uk and www.afreemind.co.uk. You can follow her on Facebook @hippocoachinguk and @afreeminduk and Twitter @hippo coaching

"If the only thing people learned was not to be afraid of their own experience, that alone would change the world."
Syd Banks

About Heart Link Charity

Heart Link was formed in 1981, as a support group for parents and families who had a child suffering with a heart defect. Over the years it has grown to be a fantastic charity supporting children and their families in many amazing ways. I've outlined, below, some of the wonderful things Heart Link has achieved but there are many more which you can read about on the website.

Parent accommodation at Glenfield hospital enabling parents to be close to their child.

Days out and family events such as Christmas parties.

Memory boxes and remembrance book for bereaved families.

Raised funds to support E.C.M.O to be introduced into the UK, now a life saving system for children and adults.

£260,000 raised to build a purpose built two storey play area, accessed directly off the paediatric cardiac ward at Glenfield Hospital.

£85,000 raised to build a helicopter pad at Glenfield Hospital to bring the sickest patients for treatment.

Caravan holidays for families whose child has a heart defect.

Heart Link Garden for quiet reflection.

Profits from the sale of this book will be donated to Heart Link. If you would like to donate further please visit the website; www.heartlink-glenfield.org.uk

Resources

Sydney Banks
www.sydbanks.com

Three Principles Global Community
www.3pgc.org

Three Principles Reseach
www.3pgc.org/evidence-of-impact

Rupert Spira
www.non-duality.rupertspira.com/home

Roger Castillio
www.rogercastillo.org

Byron Katie - The Work
www.thework.com

Adyashanti
www.adyashanti.org

Eckhart Tolle
www.eckharttolle.com

Dr. Jeffery A. Martin
The Finders book

Acknowledgments

This book would not have been possible without the beautiful contributions of the 45 writers who were willing to share their stories with you. I'm so grateful for the time, effort and the love they dedicated to this project. Many battled self doubt and anxiety about their writing and sharing their deepest secrets and I am astounded by their willingness to carry on. I know their efforts will touch lives. I love you all.

To my partner Paul, thank you for holding me accountable when I shared this book idea with you. You were never going to let me off the hook and I'm thankful for that now. Your love and support got me started and kept me going when I didn't have faith in myself. Your patience, over the years, listening to me ramble on about quantum physics, non-duality, Eastern philosophy and all things spiritual is so appreciated -some would call it heroic. I'm grateful we get to play this game of life together. I love you.

To my family and friends who have encouraged me along the way, thank you. I've had so many words of support, I particularly liked this message from Louise "Can't believe it! You are a proper grown up writer". I've also had lots of practical help - thanks to my mum for her support and doing batch cooking so the boys didn't starve when I was engulfed in the book. To MB for helping with the transcription. To Charlotte for beta reading. To Eddie, my mini guru, who shows me true nature and unconditional love in action by just being in the world. To Susan for always being there, no matter what. To Will and Jack my wonderful boys for being so perfectly you. I'm so grateful to have you all in my life. I love you all.

Thanks to Paul Locke an incredibly gifted artist who donated the beautiful image for the front cover. Paul has a deep understanding of true nature and unconditional love which he

expresses through his art. I can't tell you the excitement when Paul said I could use his work called 'Love'. I had the image from Paul before I'd even started writing the book and it spurred me on to bring the book to life. Please check his work out.
www.paullock-art.com

Thanks to Maria Iliffe-Wood who gave her time so generously to help coach and guide me through the art of self publishing. Maria is an incredible writer and coach and I'd recommend her services for any blooming authors.
www.iliffe-wood.co.uk/Services

Printed in Great Britain
by Amazon